GEORGE HENRY GERBERDING

The Way of Salvation in the Lutheran Church

First published by Just and Sinner 2020

Copyright © 2020 by George Henry Gerberding

All rights reserved. No part of this publication may be reproduced, stored or transmitted in any form or by any means, electronic, mechanical, photocopying, recording, scanning, or otherwise without written permission from the publisher. It is illegal to copy this book, post it to a website, or distribute it by any other means without permission.

Though the text this is based on is in the public domain, this edition has been heavily updated for modern readers. Inquiries may be sent to:

contact@Justandsinner.org

www.jspublishing.org

Ithaca, NY 14850

Second edition

ISBN: 978-1-952295-03-4

This book was professionally typeset on Reedsy.
Find out more at reedsy.com

Contents

Introduction — v
All Are Sinners — 1
All that is Born of Flesh Must be Born of Spirit — 5
The Present, A Dispensation of Means — 9
Baptism: A Divinely Appointed Means of Grace — 13
The Baptismal Covenant — 18
The Home — 23
Sunday School — 27
Sunday School (Part 2) — 32
Catechization — 35
The Small Catechism — 38
Teaching the Catechism — 42
Confirmation — 47
The Lord's Supper: Introduction — 52
The Lord's Supper (Part 2) — 56
The Lord's Supper (Part 3) — 60
The Confessional Service — 66
The Word as a Means of Grace — 72
Conversion: Its Nature and Necessity — 77
Varies Phenomena of Experiences — 81
Human Agency in Conversion — 87
Justification — 93
Sanctification — 100
Revivals — 106
Modern Revivals — 111
Modern Revivals (Part 2) — 118
Modern Revivals (Part 3) — 123
Revivals: The Billy Sunday Type — 130

True Revivals	133
Conclusion	142

Introduction

George Henry Gerberding was born in Pittsburgh, Pennsylvania in 1847. Though born of Lutheran parents, Gerberding was surrounded by Presbyterianism. Making sure that his children would be raised in the evangelical Lutheran faith, his father helped found the first Lutheran church in the city of Pittsburgh. There were a number of significant Lutheran figures in Western Pennsylvania at the time; most notably the eminent theologian Charles Krauth. Gerberding studied under Krauth, Henry Eyster Jacobs, and various other prominent Lutheran theologians of the time. Being immersed in a Reformed community, Gerberding saw to it that he would be able to defend his Lutheran faith in the midst of theological pluralism.

Gerberding took his first call to a small country parish in Ohio. While there, he began to encounter opposition to the Lutheran faith under the banner of revivalism which followed the "new measures" laid out by Charles Finney in the second great awakening. It was said that Christianity was primarily an experiential faith, wherein one had to have a radical conversion at some point in life. This form of Christianity denied the efficacy of the means of grace, and eschewed the historic liturgy and structure of the church. Gerberding saw to it that he would defend Lutheran faith and practice against this encroaching revivalism.

His experience with both Presbyterianism and revivalism made Gerberding able and willing to defend the Lutheran faith in a culture that viewed it as foreign and outdated. He spent nearly thirty years writing and updating *The Way of Salvation in the Lutheran Church*, the final edition being printed in 1919. This volume is an answer to revivalist Christianity which was slowly encroaching on Lutheran churches. This book was circulated widely among Lutheran churches in America, serving as instruction for both pastors and lay people to reject the unbiblical nature of revivalism. It also served to convert many to the Lutheran faith.

When reading Gerberding's work, it becomes immediately apparent that the general tenor of American Christianity has not significantly changed. The same struggles Gerberding faced, with Lutherans being labeled outdated, rote, and irrelevant to the contemporary world, are present today. If one were simply to change the names of some of the figures mentioned by Gerberding to contemporary preachers and leaders, it would come across as a contemporary book, engaging contemporary problems.

This book was not written primarily for pastors or theologians, though they will benefit immensely from reading this work. It is exceptionally readable, so that it might be used in Bible studies, Sunday school, or just read by those interested in Lutheranism or in defending their own Lutheran faith. I have encountered a few people who have mentioned to me that they became Lutheran after finding this work used somewhere, or encountering it online. I believe that a new printed edition of this work (which is long overdue) will have the same results.

In editing this work, I have sought to keep as much of the author's original language as possible, while updating phrases which are outdated or confusing. I have changed all of the Scripture references to the English Standard Version which has become perhaps the most common translation used in contemporary Lutheran resources. This will hopefully make the book more readable and engaging for congregational use. I pray that this work will speak as boldly to the twenty first century church as it did to the early twentieth.

Jordan Cooper
2013

1

All Are Sinners

WE have often heard from people who should have known better, remarks like these: "Can sinners be saved in the Lutheran Church?", or "I don't hear about any true conversions in the Lutheran Church." I have heard the comment made, more than once, that in certain churches sinners were saved, because they were converted and sanctified, but it was said to be doubtful whether anyone could find such blessings in the Lutheran Church. I also freely confess that in my early days I was surrounded by such people, and I do sympathize with those honest questioners who do not understand because they have not had the privilege of instruction in the doctrines of sin and Grace. This encouraged me to write a series of basic, practical articles on the "Way of Salvation in the Lutheran Church." It was my goal to set forth the way in which the Church of the Reformation proposes to reach the sinner, and apply to him the redemption that is in Christ Jesus.

The first question that presents itself is: Who are the subjects of salvation? The answer clearly is: All who need to be saved. Who does this embrace? The answer to this is not so unanimous. There are many different views. True, there is general agreement on this point among all the older Protestant Confessions, but the agreement is not so clear among those who claim to agree with these Confessions. In many of the denominations there is a widespread skepticism as to the reality of original sin, or inborn depravity.

Their belief is based, not on Scripture, but on their own desires. The doctrine that, "after Adam's fall, all men begotten after the common course of nature, are born with sin," is not easy to take in. It grates harshly on the human ear. It is so humbling to the pride of the human heart that people try to persuade themselves that it is not true. It has become fashionable to deny it. This happens in the pulpit, and the press, where it is denounced as unworthy of this "enlightened age." Thus the heresy has spread, and is continuing to spread. We meet people very often who stand high in their churches, and reject the idea that their children are sinners and need to be saved. Their creed is: "I believe in the purity and innocence of childhood, and in its fitness for the kingdom of heaven, without any change or application of divine Grace." Ah! yes, in some ways we would all like this to be true. But is it true? Our belief would not make it true. Then let us go "to the law and to the testimony;" to the source and fountain of all truth, the inspired Word of God. Listen to its difficult but clear statements on this topic:

What is man, that he can be pure? Or he who is born of a woman, that he can be righteous? (Job 15:14)

Behold, I was brought forth in iniquity, and in sin did my mother conceive me. (Psalm 51:5)

That which is born of the flesh is flesh, and that which is born of the Spirit is spirit. (John 3:6)

Among whom we all once lived in the passions of our flesh, carrying out the desires of the body and the mind, and were by nature children of wrath, like the rest of mankind. (Ephesians 2:3)

These are a few of the many clear, plain statements of the divine Word. Nowhere does it teach that children are born pure, righteous and fit for heaven. The Lutheran Church, then, teaches and confesses nothing but the pure truth of God's Word when the Augsburg Confession states: "Also they teach, that after Adam's fall all men, begotten after the common course of nature, are born with sin." (AC II) Also the Smalcald Articles say:

Here we must confess, that sin originated from one man Adam, by whose disobedience all were made sinners and subject to death and the devil. This is called original or capital sin . . . This hereditary sin is so deep a corruption of nature that no reason can understand it, but it must be believed from the revelation of Scripture. (SA III.I)

So also in the Formula of Concord, Chapter I., "Of Original Sin," we see a full presentation of our faith and its foundation. Also Luther's Explanation of the Second Article of the Apostles' Creed, where he says: "Who— Christ—has redeemed me, a poor, lost and condemned creature, secured and delivered me from all sins, from death, and from the power of the devil."

This then is the teaching of our Church as founded on the Word of God. That this doctrine is true, beyond the possibility of a doubt, we can learn even from our reason. It will not be disputed that what is in the child will show itself as it develops. The potential that lies hidden there will unfold and bring forth its proper and natural fruit. The nature of the child will be shown by its actions. And what are these fruits? How long will it be before that helpless and seemingly innocent baby, that sleeps on its mother's breast, will show symptoms of anger, jealousy, stubbornness and disobedience! If you leave a child to himself, and without anyone teaching him, he will learn to lie, deceive, steal, curse and give pain to others. But, without a teacher, he will not learn to pray, confess wrong, and "fear, love and trust in God above all things." Are these the symptoms and evidences of inward purity, or of inbred sin?

Again, that child is subject to sickness, suffering and death. As soon as it draws its first breath its life is a struggle. It must fight against disease. Its little body is attacked by various sicknesses. It is weakened by suffering and often experiences pain. And frequently infants even become sick unto death. How can we account for this if infants do not sin? Don't we all believe that suffering and death are the results of sin? Is there, or can there, be suffering and death where there is no sin? No infant would ever die if it were without sin. "The wages of sin is death" (Romans 6:23). But this wages is never exacted where someone has not sinned. The conclusion is irresistible. Children, even infants, are sinners. They need salvation. They need God's redeeming grace. It must be counted in. It is one of the subjects of salvation, and must be brought into the Way of Salvation.

The Church is the Bride of Christ, the institution through which Christ brings and applies this Grace to the children of men. She must begin with the child. She must reach down to the tender infant and carry the cleansing and life-giving Grace of the Redeemer even into its sin-sick soul. How is this to be done? How does the Lutheran Church propose to reach that child? Let us lay aside all our own ideas and prejudices. Let us come with an open and an unbiased mind, ready to learn and believe what God teaches and what our Church confesses.

2

All that is Born of Flesh Must be Born of Spirit

IN the former chapter we have shown, from Scripture and from reason, that our Church teaches only the plain truth of God, when she confesses that: "After Adam's fall, all men, begotten after the common course of nature, are born with sin."

As a sinful being, the new-born infant is not in the Way of Salvation. By its natural birth, from sinful parents, it is not in the kingdom of God, but in the realm and under the dominion of sin, death and the devil. If left to itself—to the undisturbed development of its own nature —it must miserably and hopelessly perish. True, there is a relative innocence. The Apostle Paul exhorts: "Therefore be imitators of God, as beloved children." (Ephesians 5:1) "Be infants in evil."(1 Corinthians 14:20) Our blessed Savior, on several occasions, rebuked the vain and ambitious spirit of the disciples by contrasting it with the spirit of a little child. He said: "To such belongs the kingdom of heaven," (Matthew 19:14) and "Truly, I say to you, unless you turn and become like children, you will never enter the kingdom of heaven." (Matthew 18:3)

But if we accept this interpretation, then the Scriptures contradict themselves; for we have seen that, in many places, they clearly teach the opposite. These passages can only mean that children are relatively innocent.

Compared with the forbidding, haughty, loveless disciples, little children are much better subjects for the kingdom. While the roots of sin are there, that sin has not yet done its hardening work.

They do not willfully resist the good. They are much more tender, docile, trustful and loving. The Grace of God has less to overcome in them. They are more easily reached, and thus are fit subjects to be brought into the kingdom of God. In this sense only can it be said, "Let the little children come to me and do not hinder them,"(Matthew 19:14) that I may touch them, bless them, impart my Grace to them, and thus make them partakers of my kingdom. "To such belongs the kingdom" (Matthew 19:14) because I desire and will to bring them into the kingdom.

We can go this far safely. We freely admit this much in favor of the child, over against the adult. But this does not mean that the child is innocent, pure and holy by nature. The undeveloped roots and germs of sin are still there. Its nature is evil. It must be saved from that moral nature.

How? Here again we meet those who claim to have a very easy solution to this problem. They say: "Admitting that the child has sin, this will in no way endanger its salvation, because Christ died to take away sin. Children have no conscious sin. Therefore, the atonement of Christ covers their case, and, without anything further, they pass into heaven, if they die in their infancy." This view seems to satisfy a lot of well-meaning people. Without thinking about it any further, they dismiss it with this seemingly easy solution. However, if they stopped to consider and examine this theory, they would see that it has no foundation. Christ's atonement alone, and in itself, never saved a soul. It removed the obstacles that were in the way of our salvation, opened the way back to our Father's house, and purchased forgiveness and salvation for us. But all this profits the sinner nothing, so long as he is not brought into that way; so long as the purchased salvation is not applied to him personally.

Neither can we say that salvation takes away the guilt of sin, but not its power. It would be to save the sinner in and with his sin. The position is utterly groundless. It is even contrary to reason. It assumes that a being who has in his heart, as a very part of his nature, the roots and germs of sin, can, with that heart unchanged, enter into the kingdom of God. It makes God look upon sin with allowance. It does violence to the holiness of His nature. It makes heaven the abode of the unclean. No, no. It will not do.

When men try to avoid what seem to them difficult and unwelcome doctrines of God's Word, they run into far worse difficulties and contradictions. That child is conceived and born in sin. It is a child of wrath, dead in trespasses and in sins. Its nature must be cleansed and renewed. Otherwise, if it can be saved as it is, there are unregenerate souls in heaven! We should live by what is written, and believe that every one, infant or adult, who has been born of the flesh, must be born of the Spirit. Listen to the earnest words of Jesus as he emphasizes them with that solemn double affirmation, "Truly, truly, I say to you, unless one is born again he cannot see the kingdom of God."(John 3:3) He repeats this sweeping declaration a second time. In the Greek it reads, "Except anyone be born again."

This statement embraces every human being. Lest this should be disputed, Jesus further says, "That which is born of the flesh" — i. e., naturally born— "is flesh, and that which is born of the Spirit is spirit."(John 3:6) Wherever there is a birth of the flesh, there must be a birth of the Spirit. The flesh-born unchanged cannot even see the kingdom of God, still less possess it, much less enjoy it. There must be new life, spiritual life, divine life breathed into that fleshly, carnal nature. Thus there will be a new heart, a new spirit, a new creature. Then, and not until then, can there be comprehension, apprehension and appreciation of the things of the kingdom of God. This is the teaching of the whole Word of God. "For neither circumcision counts for anything, nor uncircumcision, but a new creation"(Galatians 6:15)—i.e., neither Jewish birth nor Gentile birth, without the new birth. The Augsburg Confession, as quoted above, she goes on to say: "And this disease, or original fault, is truly sin, condemning and bringing eternal death upon all that are not born again." Here we must take our stand. No child can be saved unless it is first reached by renewing Grace. If an infant did ever die, or should die, in that state in which it was born, unchanged by divine Grace, that infant is lost. There are, and there can be, no unregenerate souls in heaven. Where there is no infant regeneration, there can be no infant salvation. This will be more fully explained in the next chapter.

Here also we remark, in passing, that this doctrine, of the absolute necessity of infant regeneration, is not held by the Lutheran Church alone. Even the Roman Catholic and Greek Orthodox Churches teach that it is impossible for any human creature, without a change from that condition in which he was born, to enter heaven. All the great historic confessions of the Protestant churches confess the same truth. The Calvinistic Baptists also confess the necessity of infant regeneration. In short all churches that have paid much attention to theology, and have been careful to have consistent systems of doctrine, agree on this point. However much those who call themselves by the names of these churches may deny it in their preaching and in their conversation, their own confessions of faith and their greatest and best theologians clearly teach it. Yes, there must be infant regeneration.

But is it possible? Can the Grace of God reach the helpless infant? Will He reach down and make it a new creature in Christ Jesus? Has He made provision for this end? Yes, thanks be to His abounding Grace, we believe He can and will save the child, and has committed to His spouse, the Church, a means of Grace for this purpose. He, of whom it was prophesied long before He came, that He would "gather the lambs in his arms; he will carry them in his bosom, and gently lead those that are with young" (Isaiah 40:11) who made it the first duty of the reinstated apostle to feed His lambs, must have a special care for them. It is not His or His Father's will "that one of them should perish" (Matthew 18:14). He has made provision for these sin-stricken ones, whereby His Grace can reach down to renew and heal them. There is a balm in Gilead. The Great Physician is there. The Church only needs to apply his divine, life-giving remedy.

3

The Present, A Dispensation of Means

WE have seen that the carnal, sinful nature of the child makes one unfit for the kingdom of heaven; that, therefore, there must be a change in that nature, even the birth of a new life, and the life of a new creature, before there can be either part or place in the kingdom of God. We have also expressed our firm conviction that it is the good and gracious will of God in Christ to bestow upon the poor sin-sick and unholy child the Grace needed to change it, that it might be a partaker of His great salvation. We do not think it is necessary to stop to multiply scripture passages and arguments to prove this. From beginning to end, the divine Word everywhere represents our God as a most loving, gracious, compassionate and tender Being. The tenor of the whole record is, that He delights in showing mercy, forgiving iniquity, and bestowing the Grace that brings salvation. He only punishes when justice absolutely demands it, and then reluctantly. It is not His will that any should perish.

Beyond controversy, God is willing to save the little helpless little child, apply the benefits of the atonement, impart to it the Grace of the new life, subdue the power of sin, and remove its guilt entirely. We are almost ashamed to ask such questions. And yet the humiliating fact is, that day by day, in every village and on every highway and public place of our land, we can hear men and women, professing to be Christians and calling themselves members of Christ's Church, who say that their Redeemer cannot bless a little child in this way, as to change its sinful nature! If they are hard pressed, these people, so wise in their own conceits, may admit that He can change a child's nature if He wills to, but they still feel certain that he cannot do so through His own sacrament, which was instituted for that very purpose! Thus would they limit the Holy One of Israel, and say to Omnipotence: "Thus far shall you come, and no farther"(Job 38:11).

With such people, who think themselves more wise than what is written in Scripture, knowing better than Christ, practically, even if not intentionally, charging the Son of God with folly, we do not desire controversy. Let them overthrow the very foundations of redemption if they will. Let them argue that all things are not possible with God if they dare. We still prefer to believe that the Spirit of God can change, renew and regenerate the new-born child. In Matthew 3:9, we read: "For I tell you, God is able from these stones to raise up children for Abraham,"—i.e., as the connection shows, spiritual children of Abraham, true children of God. We may not be able to understand the process by which God could change the rough, hard stones of the field into true children of God, but we believe it, because the Word says so. And because we believe that, it is not hard for us to believe that He can impart His own divine life to the heart of the child, and thus make it a new creature in Christ Jesus.

He could, if it so pleased Him, do it without any means. God could recreate the human soul by a mere act of His will. He could do so by a word, as He created the universe. Without the contact of any outward means, without directly bringing His Word to them in any way, Christ healed the ruler's son and the daughter of the Syro-Phenician woman. But if He can do this without means, who will say that He cannot do the same thing through means? Since, then, He can accomplish his own purposes of Grace either with or without means, it only remains for us to ask: in what way has it pleased God to work? Does He in the present time work mediately or immediately? It will hardly be disputed that the present is a dispensation of means—that even in the domain of nature, and much more in the realm of Grace, He ordinarily carries out His purposes through means.

He chooses His own means. They may sometimes seem foolish to humans, especially in the operations of His Grace. Our Savior, in working miracles, used some means that must have struck those interested as very unusual. "Having said these things, he spit on the ground and made mud with the saliva. Then he anointed the man's eyes with the mud"(John 9:6). Well might the blind man have said: "What good can a little dirt mixed with spit do?" Yet it pleased our Lord to use it as a means, in working that stupendous miracle.

When Jesus asked for the five barley loaves and two small fish to feed the five thousand, even an apostle said: "What good are these among so many?" Yes, what are they? In the hands of a mere man nothing—even worse than nothing; only enough to taunt the hungry thousands and a cause for people to become angry. But in the hands of the Son of God, with His blessing on them, taken from His hands, and distributed according to His Word they became a feast in the wilderness.

A poor woman, a sufferer for twelve years, craves healing from our Lord. With a woman's faith, timid though strong, she presses through the crowd close up to Jesus, and with her trembling bony fingers touches the hem of His garment. Jesus perceives that virtue is gone out of Him. The woman perceives that virtue, healing and life are come into her. There was a transfer from Christ's blessed life-giving body, into the diseased suffering body of the woman. And what was the medium of the transfer? The fringe of His garment—a piece of cloth. Yes, if it so pleases the mighty God, the everlasting Savior, He can use a piece of cloth as a means to transfer healing and life from himself to someone who is suffering. That same Savior still works through means. He has founded a Church, ordained a ministry, and instituted the preaching of the Word and the administration of His own sacraments.

Christ now works in and through His Church. Through her ministry, preaching the Word, and administering the sacraments, the Holy Spirit is given. (Augsburg Confession, Article 5). When Christ sent forth His apostles to make disciples of all nations, He instructed them how they were to do it. The great commission reads: "All authority in heaven and on earth has been given to me. Go therefore and make disciples of all nations, baptizing them in the name of the Father and of the Son and of the Holy Spirit, teaching them to observe all that I have commanded you. And behold, I am with you always, to the end of the age" (Matthew 28:18-20). Here then are the Savior's explicit instructions. The Apostles are to make disciples. This is the object of their mission. How are they to do it? By baptizing them into the name of the triune God, and teaching them to observe all Christ's commands. This is Christ's own appointed way of applying His Grace to sinful men, and bringing them out of a state of sin into a state of grace. And this is the Way of Salvation in the Lutheran Church.

We begin with the child, who needs Grace. We begin by baptizing that child into Christ. Therefore, we lay a lot of stress on baptism. We teach our people that it is sinful, if not perilous, to neglect the baptism of their children. The Lutheran Church attaches more importance to this divine ordinance than does any other Protestant Church. While all around us there has been a weakening and yielding on this point; while the spirit of our age and country scorns the idea of a child receiving divine Grace through baptism; while it has become offensive to the popular ear to speak of baptismal Grace, our Church, wherever she has been and is true to herself, stands today where Martin Luther and his co-workers stood, where the confessors of Augsburg stood, and where the framers of the Book of Concord stood.

The world still asks: "What good can a little water do?" We answer, first of all: "Baptism is not simply water, but it is the water comprehended in God's command and connected with God's Word" (Luther's Small Catechism). The Lutheran Church knows of no baptism that is only "a little water." We can't speak of such a baptism. Understand that when we speak of baptism, we speak of it as defined above, by Luther. We cannot separate the water from the Word. We would not dare to baptize with water without the Word. In the words of Luther, that would be "simply water, and no baptism." Keep in mind that whatever benefits and effects we ascribe to baptism, in the further clear words of Luther's Catechism: "It is not the water, indeed, that produces these effects, but the Word of God which accompanies and is connected with the water, and our faith which relies on the Word of God connected with the water." If someone asks further: "What good can baptism as you defined it do?" We will try to answer, or, rather, we will let God's Word answer. "What do the Scriptures say?"

4

Baptism: A Divinely Appointed Means of Grace

WHEN we look into the benefits and blessings which the Word of God connects with baptism we must be careful to receive the true meaning and necessary reading of its statements. We can't take isolated passages, apply whatever meaning to them we see fit, and then build our doctrine on that basis. In this way the Holy Scriptures have been made to teach and support the worst errors and most dangerous heresies. In this way many people "twist the Scriptures to their own destruction"(2 Peter 3:16). On this important point our Church has laid down certain plain, practical, safe and sound principles. By keeping in mind, and following these fundamental directions, in the interpretation of the divine Word, the most uneducated reader of the Scriptures can save himself from confusion, perplexity and doubt.

One of the first and most important principles, insisted on by our theologians and the writers of our Confessions, is that a passage of Scripture is always to be taken in its natural, plain and literal sense, be studied in its context, in connection with what is written before and after it. Again—and this is of an extremely important point—Scripture is to be interpreted by Scripture. As Quenstedt says: "Passages which need explanation can and should be explained by other passages that are more clear, and thus the

Scripture itself furnishes an interpretation of obscure expressions, when a comparison of these is made with those that are more clear. So that Scripture is explained by Scripture." According to these principles, we should not say that anything is Biblical until we have studied the complete Scriptural testimony to the subject.

In this manner then we wish to answer the question: What is written about the benefits and blessings given in baptism? We have already referred to the commission given to the Apostles in Matthew 28:19. We have seen that in that commission our Lord makes baptism one of the means through which the Holy Spirit makes disciples.

In Mark 16:16, he says: "He that believes and is baptized will be saved." In John 3:5, he says: "Unless one" — i.e., any one— "is born of water and the Spirit, he cannot enter the kingdom of God." In Acts 2:38, the Apostle says: "Repent and be baptized every one of you in the name of Jesus Christ for the forgiveness of your sins."

Also,

Arise and be baptized, and wash away your sins, calling on his name (Acts 22:16).

Do you not know that all of us who have been baptized into Christ Jesus were baptized into his death? (Romans 6:3)

As many of you as were baptized into Christ have put on Christ (Galatians 3:27).

Christ loved the Church and gave himself for her, that he might sanctify her, having cleansed her by the washing of water with the word (Ephesians 5:25-26).

Having been buried with him in baptism, in which you were also raised with him through faith in the powerful working of God, who raised him from the dead (Colossians 2:12).

He saved us, not because of works done by us in righteousness, but according to his own mercy, by the washing of regeneration and renewal of the Holy Spirit (Titus 3:5).

Baptism, which corresponds to this, now saves you, not as a removal of dirt from the body but as an appeal to God for a good conscience, through the resurrection of Jesus Christ (1 Peter 3:21).

There are a few other passages in which baptism is merely mentioned, but not explained. There is not one passage that teaches anything different from those quoted here. All we ask of the reader is to examine these passages carefully to compare them one with the other and to ask himself: What do they teach? What is the meaning which a plain, unprejudiced reader, who has implicit confidence in the Word and the power of God, would derive from them. Can he say, "Baptism doesn't do anything?" "It is of no consequence." "It's just a Church ceremony, without any particular blessing in it." Or, do the words clearly teach that it is nothing more than a sign—an outward sign—of an invisible grace? Look again at the expressions of these passages. We want to be clear here, because this is one of the points on which the Lutheran Church today differs from others.

Jesus mentions water as well as Spirit, when speaking of the new birth. "Make disciples, (by) baptizing them." "Be baptized for the remission of your sins." "Be baptized and wash away your sins." "Baptized into Christ." By baptism "put on Christ." Christ designs to sanctify and cleanse the Church with "the washing of water by the Word." " Washing of regeneration and renewal of the Holy Spirit." "Baptism now saves you." The language is certainly strong and clear. Any principle of interpretation, by which baptismal Grace and regeneration can be eliminated from these passages, will overthrow every doctrine of our holy Christian faith.

Our Catechism here also teaches nothing but the pure truth of the Word, when it asserts that baptism "works forgiveness of sins, delivers from death and the devil, and confers everlasting salvation on all who believe, as the Word and promise of God declare." Our firm and impenetrable Augsburg Confession, also, in Article II confesses that the new birth by baptism and the Holy Spirit delivers from the power and penalty of original sin.

Also in Article IX.: "Of baptism they teach that it is necessary to salvation, and that by baptism the Grace of God is offered, and that children are to be baptized, who by baptism are being offered to God are received into God's favor." The question may be asked, "is baptism so absolutely essential to salvation, that unbaptized children are all lost?" To this we would briefly reply, that the people who wrote our Confessions deny emphatically that it is absolutely necessary. Luther, Melanchthon, Bugenhagen and others, repudiate the idea that an unbaptized infant is lost. No single acknowledged theologian of the Lutheran Church ever taught this repulsive doctrine.

Why then does our Confession say baptism is necessary to salvation? It is necessary in the same sense in which it is necessary to use all Christ's ordinances. The necessity is ordinary, not absolute. Ordinarily Christ bestows His Grace on the child through baptism, as the means or channel through which the Holy Spirit is conferred. But when, through no fault of its own, this is not applied, He can reach the infant in some other way. As we have seen above, He is not so limited to certain means that His Grace cannot operate without them. The only thing our Church insists on in the case of a child as absolutely necessary, is the new birth. Ordinarily this is effected, by the Holy Spirit, through baptism, as the means of Grace. When the means, however, cannot be or, through no fault of the child, are not applied, the Spirit of God can effect this new birth in some other way. He is not bound to means. And from what we have learned above of the will of God toward these little ones we have every reason to believe that He does so reach and change every infant that dies unbaptized.

The position of our Church, as accepted by all her great theologians, was clearly expressed by Augustine in the words, "Not the absence but the contempt of the sacrament condemns." It is not the child but the parents who are responsible for the absence of the Sacrament. The guilt is on the parents. While the Lutheran Church, therefore, has confidence enough in her dear heavenly Father and loving Savior, to believe that her Lord will never let a little one perish, but will always regenerate and fit it for His blessed Kingdom, she still insists on having the children of all her households baptized into Christ. It can't be simply a matter of indifference to deprive an infant of the means of grace.

Others say that there is no command in the Bible to baptize infants. Without giving an extensive answer, we can say briefly: It is enough for a Lutheran to know that the divine commission is to "baptize the nations" —there never was a nation without infants. The children need Grace: baptism confers Grace. It is specially adapted to impart spiritual blessings to these little ones. We can't take the preached Word, but we can take the sacramental Word and apply it to them. God established infant membership in his Church. He alone has a right to revoke it. He has never done so. Therefore it stands.

If the Old Testament covenant of Grace embraced infants, the New is not narrower, but wider. The pious Baptist mother's heart is much more scripturally correct than her head. She presses her baby to her breast, and prays to Jesus that he would bless that child. She knows and believes in her heart that her dear child needs the blessing of Jesus, and that He can bestow the needed blessing. And yet she will deny that He can bless it through His own sacrament— "the washing of water by the Word." The devout Lutheran mother presses her baptized child to her bosom, looks into its eyes, and thanks her Savior from the depth of her heart, that He has blessed her child; that He has breathed into it His divine life, washed it, sealed it, and adopted it as His son or daughter. How sweet is the consolation of knowing that her precious little one is a lamb of Christ's flock, "bearing on its body the marks of the Lord Jesus." But Christian parents have not fulfilled their whole duty when they have had their children baptized into Christ. The children certainly are now in covenant relationship with Jesus Christ. But it is the duty and blessed privilege of the parents to keep their little ones in that covenant of Grace.

5

The Baptismal Covenant

The Baptismal Covenant Can Be Kept Unbroken. The Aim and Responsibility of Parents

WE have gone "to the Law and to the Testimony" to find out what the nature and benefits of Baptism are. We have gathered out of the Word all the most important passages about this subject. We have grouped them together and have studied them side by side. We have observed that they all agree with one another, and are rather clear. Unless we are willing to throw aside all sound principles of interpretation, we can take only one meaning from the inspired words, and that is that the baptized child is, by virtue of that divine ordinance, a new creature in Christ Jesus.

Here let us be careful, however, to bear in mind and keep before us that we claim for the child only the birth of a new life. It has been born of water and the Spirit. A birth we know is a very feeble beginning of an independent life. So faint are the flickerings of the natural life at birth, that it's often doubtful whether any life is present. The little child needs the most tender, watchful and intelligent fostering and care. So is it also in the Kingdom of Grace. The divine life is there. But it is life in its first beginnings. As yet there is only the seed and germ of the new life. And this young spiritual life also needs gentle fostering and careful nourishing. Like the natural life of the child, so its spiritual life is full of perils. While the beginnings of the new life are there, we must not forget that the roots of sin are also still there. Our Church does not teach with Borne that "sin (original) is destroyed in baptism, so that it no longer exists." Hollazius says: "The guilt and dominion of sin is taken away by baptism, but not the root or tinder of sin." Luther also writes that "Baptism takes away the guilt of sin, although the material, called concupiscence, remains." Unfortunately for the child these roots of sin will grow of their own accord, like the weeds in our gardens. They do not need fostering care. Not so with the germs of the new life. They, like the most precious plants of the gardens, must be watched and guarded and tended continually.

Solomon says: Prov. 29:15, "The rod and reproof give wisdom, but a child left to himself brings shame to his mother." And this is only too often true even of a baptized child. The Christian parent, therefore, has not fulfilled his whole duty to the child when he has had it baptized. It is now the parents' duty; or rather it should be considered the parents' most blessed privilege to keep that child in covenant relationship with the blessed Redeemer. This also belongs to the teaching of the Church of the Reformation.

This point, however, many parents seem to forget. Many who are sound on the question of baptismal Grace, are very unsound as to a parent's duty to the baptized child. Hunnius, a recognized standard theologian of our Church, in speaking of the responsibility of those who present children for baptism says it is expected of them: First, to answer, in behalf of the child, as to the faith in which it is to be baptized, and in which it is to be brought up. Second, to instruct the child when it comes to years of discretion, that it has been truly baptized, as Christ has commanded. Third, to pray for the child, that God may keep it in the covenant of grace and bless it in body and spirit, and finally to preserve it with all true believers. Fourth, to use all diligence that the child may grow up in that faith, which they have confessed in the child's name, and thus be preserved from dangerous error and false doctrine.

That most delightful Lutheran theologian, Luthardt, says: " Infant baptism is a comfort beyond any other, but it is also a responsibility beyond any other." Again:

As Christians we know that God has bestowed upon our children not only natural, but spiritual gifts. For our children have been baptized and received by baptism into the Covenant of Grace. To preserve them in this baptismal Grace, to develop in them the life of God's spirit, this is one side of Christian education. To contend against sin in the child is the other.

Dr. Schmid, in his Christian Ethics, also teaches that it is possible to continue in the uninterrupted enjoyment of baptismal Grace. Dr. Pontoppidan, in his excellent explanation of Luther's Small Catechism, asks the question: "Is it possible to keep one's baptismal covenant?" He answers: "Yes, by the Grace of God it is possible." The teaching of our Church, therefore, is that the baptized child can grow up a child of Grace from infancy and that, under God, it rests primarily with the parents or guardians.

And this Lutheran idea, like all others, is grounded in the Word of God. We note a few examples: Samuel was a child of prayer, given to his pious mother in answer to prayer. She called him Samuel, i.e., asked of God. Even before his birth she dedicated him to God. As soon as he was weaned she carried him to the Tabernacle and there publicly consecrated him to the service of the Most High. From this time forth, according to the sacred record, he dwelt in God's Tabernacle and "ministered unto the Lord before Eli." As a mere child God used him as a prophet. Of the prophet Jeremiah it is written: (Jeremiah 1:5) "Before you were born I consecrated you." Of John the Baptist it is written: (Luke 1:15) "He will be filled with the Holy Spirit, even from his mother's womb." To Timothy, Paul says: "from childhood you have been acquainted with the sacred writings, which are able to make you wise for salvation through faith in Christ Jesus," (2 Timothy 3:15) and: "For you, O Lord, are my hope,

my trust, O LORD, from my youth. Upon you I have leaned from before my birth; you are he who took me from my mother's womb" (Psalm 71:5-6).

It is therefore possible for God not only to give His Grace to a child but to keep that child in His Grace all its days. To dispute this is, simply, to dispute the record that God gave. Lest someone should still say, however, that the examples above noted are isolated and exceptional, we note further, that the tenor of the whole Word is in agreement with this idea. Nowhere in the whole Bible is it even intimated that it is God's desire or plan that children must remain outside of the covenant of Grace, and have no part or lot in the benefits of Christ's redeeming work until they come to years of discretion and can choose for themselves. This modern idea is utterly foreign and contradictory to all we know of God, of His scheme of redemption, and of His dealings with His people, either in the old or new covenants.

He ordained that infants at eight days old should be brought into His covenant. He recognized infant children as partakers of the blessings of His covenant. "Out of the mouth of infants and nursing babies you have prepared perfect praise;"(Matthew 21:16) "Let the little children come to me and do not hinder them"(Matthew 19:14). Everywhere it is taken for granted that the children who have received either the Old or New Testament sacrament of initiation are His.

Parents are nowhere told that they should try and convert their children, as if they had not already received grace. But everywhere they are exhorted to keep them in that relation to their Lord, into which His own ordinance has brought them.

For I have chosen him, that he may command his children and his household after him to keep the way of the LORD by doing righteousness and justice, so that the LORD may bring to Abraham what he has promised him (Genesis 18:19).

That the next generation might know them, the children yet unborn, and arise and tell them to their children, so that they should set their hope in God and not forget the works of God, but keep his commandments; (Psalm 76:6-7).

Train up a child in the way he should go; even when he is old he will not depart from it (Proverbs 22:6).

Fathers, do not provoke your children to anger, but bring them up in the discipline and instruction of the Lord (Ephesians 6:4).

Let the baptized child then be looked upon as already belonging to Christ. The germs of faith and love are there.

If the parent appreciates this fact and does his part, confidence and trust in

Christ, and the purest love to God will be developed early. From the seed of faith will grow the beautiful plant of child-trust and child-love. The graces of the new life may be thus early drawn out, so that the child in later years will never know of a time when it did not trust and love, and as a result of this love hate sin. This is the ideal of God's Word. It is the ideal which every Christian parent should strive to realize in the children given by God, and given to God in His own ordinance. Can it be done?

6

The Home

Home Influence and Training in Their Relation to The Keeping Of The Baptismal Covenant

ACCORDING to the last chapter, it is indeed a high and holy ideal that every Christian parent should set before him in regard to his children. Every Christian child should be treated as a son or daughter of God from the moment of their baptism. The child is to be so fostered and nurtured and trained that, from the time it is self-conscious, it is to grow day by day in knowledge and in Grace. As it grows in body, so it is to increase in wisdom and in favor with God and with man. In order that this may happen, it is first of all necessary that there be the proper surroundings.

We can't expect that parent to draw out these graces of the new life in the child, who is not himself imbued with a spirit of living faith and fervent love to Christ. In the beautiful words of Luthardt:

Religion must first approach the child in the form of life, and afterward in the form of instruction. Let religion be the atmosphere by which the child is surrounded, the air which it breathes. The spirit of the home, its order, its practice—that world in which the child finds himself so soon as he knows himself—this it is which must make religion appear to him a thing natural and self-evident.

And this is especially important for the mother. It is while resting on the mother's breast and playing at the mother's knee, that the child is receiving impressions that become stones for character building. The father, of course, is not released from responsibility. He too is to set a holy example, to make impressions for good and to use all his influence to direct the thoughts and inclinations of the child upward. The man who does not help in the religious training of his own children is not fit to be a father. But it is after all with the mother that the little child spends most of its time and receives most of its impressions. Oh, that every mother were a Hannah, an Elizabeth, an Eunice. Then would there be more Samuels, Johns and Timothys.

Let us have more of the spirit of Christ in the heart of the mother and father, and in the home. Let the child learn, with the beginings of self-consciousness, that Jesus is known and loved and honored in the home, and there will be little or no trouble about the future. But the child must be instructed. Begin early. Let it learn to pray as soon as it can speak. Let it use its first lispings and stammerings in speaking words of prayer. We quote again from Luthardt:

Let it not be objected that the child cannot understand the prayer. The way of education is by practice to understanding, not by understanding to practice. And the child will have a feeling and a presentiment of what it cannot understand. The world of heavenly things is not an incomprehensible region to the child, but the home of its spirit. The child will speak to his Father in Heaven without needing much instruction as to who that Father is. It seems as though God were a well-known friend of his heart. The child will love to pray. If mother forgets it, the child will not.

Therefore, oh, you parents! pray for your child. Pray with your child. Teach that child to pray. The writer knows of a little girl who came home from Sunday-school and said: "Mamma, why don't you ever be sanctified, i. e., made more and more holy "through the truth." As a child it needs first the "milk of the Word." It is not desirable, neither is it necessary, to try to teach the very young child doctrines and abstract truths. Neither ought the child to be required to learn by rote long passages from the Scriptures. In this way some well-meaning but mistaken parents make the Word a burden to their children, and it becomes odious in their eyes. There are other and better ways.

Begin by showing the child Bible pictures, even if it should soil the book a little. Better a thousand times have the lessons of life and love from the old Bible graven on the heart of the child, than to have its fine engravings as a parlor ornament for strangers. In our day there is also an abundant supply of Bible pictures and story books for children. Those parents who have never tried it will be surprised to see the interest the little ones will take in these. Connect the pictures with the stories of the Bible. And what stories are better to teach children than those that have been used for generations? When will children ever be tired of hearing of Joseph, and Moses, and David, and Daniel, and especially of Him who is the special Friend of children? It will be easy to so connect the teachings of the Word with these pictures and stories that very young children will be able to distinguish right from wrong, to know and hate sin, and to be drawn ever nearer to the blessed Jesus.

As they become able to study, to think and to comprehend it, the judicious parent will be glad to avail himself of the help of Luther's Catechism. Here the more important teachings of the Word are summarized and systematized. Most parents indeed shirk this duty, and flatter themselves that if they send their children to catechetical class when they grow old enough they have performed their whole duty. Such parents do not perhaps know that Martin Luther wrote his Small Catechism especially for family use. Let them take their Church Books and turn to the Catechism, and they will find that Luther heads the Ten Commandments with the words: "In the plain form in which they are to be taught by the head of the family." So also with the Creed, the Lord's Prayer, and the Sacraments. This is Luther's idea. It is the true idea. It belongs to the Way of Salvation in the Lutheran Church. It is the custom, still practiced in our older Lutheran churches.

The pastor, as we shall see, is only to help the parents, and not to do everything for them. The teaching of the Catechism at home will give the parents an opportunity to speak of and to explain what sin is, what faith is, what prayer is, and what the sacraments are. We would impress also the importance of instructing the child concerning its own baptism. Let it understand not only the fact of its baptism, but the nature, benefits and obligations of the same. It certainly has a most salutary effect to impress the thought on the child frequently that it was given to Christ and belongs to Him—that He has received it as His own, and adopted it into the family of the redeemed.

Here also there is a sad neglect on the part of parents. Many never say a word to their children about their baptism. Many children even grow up and know not whether they are baptized or not. This is certainly un-Scriptural and un-Lutheran. "Do you not know," says Paul, as if he said, have you forgotten it? "that all of us who have been baptized into Christ Jesus have been baptized into his death?" (Romans 6:3). Doubtless if we appreciated our own baptism as we should, it would be a constant source of comfort, a never-failing fountain of Grace to us, and to our children.

The Apostles frequently speak of the "Church that is in the house." By this they mean such a household as we have tried to portray—a home where the religion of our blessed Savior permeates the whole atmosphere; where the Word of God dwells richly; where there are altars of prayer and closets for prayer —a home where Jesus is a daily well-known Guest; where the children, baptized into Christ, are nourished with the milk of the Word, so that they grow in it, increasing more and more, growing up unto Him who is the Head, even Christ. In such a home the Church is in the house, and the household in the Church. Blessed home! Blessed children, who have such parents! No anxious, restless parents who are hoping and praying that their children may be converted. No confused, repelled children there, crying because Jesus will not love them till they "get religion." On the contrary, parents and children, kneeling at one altar, children of one Father, with the same trust, the same hope, the same Lord—hand in hand they go from the church in the house to the house of God's Church. Says Dr. Cuyler, an eminent Presbyterian, "The children of Christian parents ought never to need conversion."

7

Sunday School

The Sunday School In Its Relation To The Baptized Children Of Christian Parents.

WE have tried to set forth the Lutheran idea of a Christian home. In such a home, called, "a Church in the House," all ought to be Christians. The children having been given and consecrated to Christ in holy baptism, and having had His renewing and life-giving Grace imparted to them through that Sacrament, are to be kept in that relationship with Him. The popular idea that they must of necessity, during the most impressible and important period of their existence, belong to the world, the flesh and the devil, is utterly foreign to the Lutheran, or Scriptural view. That the child is fated, for a number of years, to be under the influence of evil, and to be permitted to "sow wild oats" before divine Grace can reach it, is certainly a principle that is contradictory to the whole scheme of salvation. Yet this seems to be the idea of those parents who will not believe that God can reach it, is certainly a principle that is contradictory to the Way of Salvation. These people treat their children much as a farmer does his colts, letting them run wild for a while, and then violently breaking them in.

This pernicious idea has also obtained sway to an alarming extent in the Sunday-school system of our land. The children in the Sunday-school, whether baptized or not, whether from Christian or from Christless homes, are looked upon as outsiders, impenitent sinners, utter strangers to Christ and His Grace, until they experience such a marked change that they can tell exactly where and when and how they were converted. Hence the popular idea that it is the object of the Sunday-School to convert the children.

This seems to be the underlying principle of both the American Sunday-school Union and the American Tract Society; institutions otherwise so excellent that it is hard to say anything against either. This idea pervades also the undenominational helps and comments of the International Lesson System. This is the undertone of the great mass of undenominational Sunday-school music. It is the key-note of the County, State, National and International Sunday-school Conventions and Institutes. This idea is so popular and wide-spread that many Lutheran pastors, Sundays school teachers and workers have unconsciously bought into it. Even some of our own Church papers, sometimes publish articles setting forth the idea that it is the object of the Sunday-school to Christianize the children. As though the baptized children of the Church, the children of devout Christian parents, had been heathen, until Christianized by the Sunday-school! Some of our old Sunday school constitutions also set it down as the object of the school to "lead the children to Christ," or to "labor for their conversion."

Now we believe that this idea is un-biblical and therefore un-Lutheran. If what we have written in the preceding chapters on baptismal Grace, the baptismal covenant, and the possibility of keeping that covenant, is true, then this popular idea is false. And vice versa, if this popular view is correct, then the whole Lutheran teaching of baptism, baptismal Grace, and the baptismal covenant must fall to the ground.

But despite the constant opposition, we still believe this is the pure teaching of God's word. Where we have the "Church in the House," there we have lambs of Christ's flock. Ah, how many more we could have, how many more we would have, if the fathers and mothers in the Church understood this precious article of our faith, and prayerfully built their home life on this! Then would there be a more regular and healthful growth of the Church, and the necessity for fitful, spasmodic revival efforts would stop.

From our Christian homes the baptized children of the Church come to the Sunday-school. How is the school to treat them?—We are talking now of the baptized children from Christian homes; we will talk about the unbaptized and untrained further on. These children, with all their childish waywardness and restlessness, do generally love Jesus. They do trust in Him, and are unhappy when they know that they have committed a sin against Him. They do, when taught, pray to Him, believe that He hears their prayers and. loves them. Shall the teacher now begin to impress upon the minds and hearts of these little ones the idea that they are not yet Christ's, and that Christ has nothing to do with them, except to seek and call them, until they are converted? And shall they go home from Sunday-school with the impression that all their prayers have been empty and useless, because their hearts have not been changed? Dare the Sunday-school thus confuse the child, raise doubts as to Christ's forgiveness and love, and "quench the Spirit?" Oh how sad, that thus thousands of children have their first love, their first trust, quenched by those who have more zeal than knowledge.

No, no, these are Christ's lambs. They come with His marks upon them. Let the Sunday school teacher work in harmony with the mother who gave these children to Christ. Let the whole atmosphere of the school impress on that child the precious truth that it is Jesus' little lamb. Feed that lamb, feed it with the sincere milk of the Word. Lead that lamb gently; teach it to understand its relation to the Great Shepherd, to know Him, to rejoice in His love, to love His voice, to follow His leadings more and more closely, instead of singing miserably:

I am young, but I must die,
In my grave I soon shall lie.
Am I ready now to go,
If the will of God be so?
or,
When saints gather round Thee, dear Savior above, And hasten to crown Thee with jewels of love,
Amid those bright mansions of glory so fair—
Oh, tell me, dear Savior, if I shall be there!

Some of these sentiments are unscriptural. Some may do for grown up penitent prodigals. But all are out of place on the lips of the baptized children of the Church. Let such rather joyfully sing:

I am Jesus' little lamb,
Therefore glad and gay I am;
Jesus loves me, Jesus knows me,
All that's good and fair He shows me,
Tends me every day the same,
Even calls me by my name,

and such other cheerful and healthy hymns that breathe the spirit of the Church of the Reformation. This we believe to be the object of our Sunday-schools, as far as the baptized children of Christian parents are concerned. They are to be helps, to keep the children true to their baptismal covenant, and to enable them to grow strong and ever stronger against sin and in holiness. Jesus did not tell Peter to convert, but to feed His sheep.

From this, we see how important it is to have Lutheran Sunday-school teachers who "know whether the teaching is from God;" (John 7:17) who are "built up in him and established in the faith;" (Colossians 2:7) who are "always prepared to make a defense to anyone who asks for a reason for the hope that is within them;"(1 Peter 3:15) who are "able to teach"(2 Timothy 2:24). A teacher who does not understand and appreciate the Lutheran doctrine of baptism is out of place in a Lutheran Sunday-school. It is certainly not desirable to have the child instructed at home that it was given to Christ in baptism, received and owned by Him and belongs to Him, and then have the Sunday-school teacher teach it that until it experiences some remarkable change, which the teacher cannot at all explain, it belongs not to Christ, but to the unconverted world. The teaching of the pulpit, the catechetical class, the home and the Sunday-school, ought certainly to be in perfect harmony—especially so on the vital point of the personal relation of the child to the Savior and His salvation. To have clashing and contradictory instruction is a sure way to sow the seeds of doubt and skepticism.

We must have sound instruction and influence in the Sunday-school, and to this end we must have sound and clear helps and equipment for teacher and student. The worship of the school, the singing, the opening and closing exercises, must all be in harmony with this great fundamental idea of feeding those who are Christ's lambs.

8

Sunday School (Part 2)

The Sunday School—Its Relation To Those In Covenant Relationship With Christ, And Also To The Unbaptized And Wandering.

WE are still discussing how Sunday-school deals with the baptized children of Christian parents. We have seen how important it is that the Sunday-school work in harmony with the pastor and the parent. We have seen that, to this end, it is especially important that the instruction of the teacher is in harmony with the doctrine of our Church on baptismal Grace, and the keeping of the baptismal covenant. Here, however, we meet with a practical difficulty. Too many of our teachers are not clear themselves on this subject. Their own early instruction may have been imperfect. Their whole environment may have been unfavorable to rooting and grounding them in this faith, once delivered to the saints. This old-fashioned faith, as we have seen, has become uncommon in many localities and circles, and to profess this faith is to invite ridicule and opposition. The Lutheran Church in this matter, as in others, is considered behind the age, because the age is away ahead of Christ and the Apostles, the Church Fathers and the Reformers. What wonder then that in many places, our members, on whom we must depend for teachers, have unconsciously drifted away from the old landmarks, and are altogether at sea as to God's means and methods of Grace, especially with the children? It is, therefore, a matter of the gravest importance that our Church place in the hands of her willing but inexperienced teachers such plain, practical and full helps and equipment as will enable them to be safe and successful instructors in our Sunday-schools.

Our good teachers are always willing to learn. They need to be and want to be first taught. They need clear, sound exposition, illustration and application of every lesson for themselves, before they can successfully teach others. They need to be shown in every lesson how the divine Word everywhere sets forth the great doctrines of our church.

We have only spoken so far about those children who are baptized Christians, but there are some who have already wandered away. There are children who have never been either baptized or instructed in heavenly things. Or, if baptized, they have been permitted to grow up afterwards as wild as heathen children. Yes, even in the homes of members of our own Church, there are children, whether baptized or not, who are thus growing up utterly neglected. If baptized, they do not even know it. Much less do they know the significance of their baptism.[1] It is the mission of the Sunday-school to gather in these destitute ones, from the street, and from their Christless homes. This is one effectual form of Lutheran Evangelism. The Sunday-school must become a spiritual home for them. The earnest teacher can and ought to find out who of his pupils belong to this class, and apply to such the needed instruction and exhortation. In their case it is truly the object of the Sunday-school to lead them to Jesus, to labor for were baptized, and perhaps also, to some extent, instructed in divine things, but who have gone astray, and have thus fallen from their baptismal covenant. All such, who are not at present in covenant relationship with Christ, who are turned away from Christ, must be turned back, i. e., converted.

Now this difficult work, this great change, can be accomplished only through the power of God's Word. "The law of the Lord is perfect, reviving

---

[1] See Problems and Possibilities p. 103 ff. and also Chapter X of same book.

the soul"(Psalm 19:7). The Gospel of Christ is "the power of God unto salvation"(Romans 1:16). The words of Christ, "they are spirit and life"(John 6:63). If sinners, whether young or old, are to be reclaimed for Christ, it must be through that Word which "is living" — i.e., full of life— "and active, sharper than any two-edged sword"(Hebrews 4:12). Let the Sunday-school teacher depend on nothing else than this Word of God. It is always accompanied by the Spirit of God. It is the living soul of the new life. Let it be used prayerfully. Let it be taught carefully. Let it be taught clearly. Let it be impressed and applied to heart, and conscience, and life. Drive it home personally and individually to the impenitent pupil. See him by himself, visit him in his home, teach him in his class. Cease not your prayers and your efforts till the Word so lodge and fasten itself in the mind and conscience that it makes him realize his own sinfulness and his need of a Savior, and also that Savior's readiness to save. This is God's way of salvation. This is the Way of Salvation in the Lutheran Church.

The Sunday-school teacher who follows this way will win souls. The impenitent sinners of his class will be brought to repentance toward God, and faith in our Lord Jesus Christ; or in one word, they will be converted; while those who are already Christ's will grow in Grace and in the knowledge of our Lord and Savior Jesus Christ. Where this is faithfully and persistently done there the Sunday-school teacher is doing a truly scriptural and a most blessed evangelistic work. Let us have more of it. It is sorely needed in city, in village and in the open country.

9

Catechization

WE have spoken of the importance and benefits of home training and instruction. We endeavored to show that Christian parents are under the most solemn obligation to instruct their children in the truth of God's Word. We also endeavored to show that, in order to give their children a clear understanding of the saving truths of the Bible, they could do no better than to diligently teach them Luther's Small Catechism; that this was really Luther's idea and purpose when he wrote that excellent little religious manual; that the first catechetical class ought indeed to be in the family, with father and mother as teachers;—that this home class ought to be carried on so long and so persistently, that in it the children would become perfectly familiar with the contents of the book; so familiar indeed, that they would know all the parts that Luther wrote perfectly by heart. Luther's Small Catechism, i.e., the parts that Luther wrote himself, is really quite a small book.

By giving only a little time and attention to it each week, the parents could easily, in a few years, have all their children know it as well as their multiplication table. And such ought to be the case. After these beginnings have thus been made, and while the home instruction is still going on, the work of the Sunday-school teacher comes in as a help to the home class. In every Sunday-school class there ought to be, with each lesson, some instruction in the Catechism. To this end each teacher, in a Lutheran Sunday-school, ought to be familiarly at home in this most important text-book. The teacher should endeavor so to teach these lessons that the pupil would learn to love and appreciate the Catechism more and more. Thus, the school ought to be a helper to the home.

And thus, home and school together, working in harmony for the same end, would prepare the children for the pastor's catechetical class. If this good old-fashioned custom were kept up in all our households and schools, then would the pastor's catechetical class be more of a pleasure and a profit to himself and his catechumens. It would then be the pastor's part, as it should be, to review the contents with his class, and thus to find how well the preparatory work had been done. Then he could devote his time and energy to what should be really the pastor's part of the work, viz., to explain and set forth clearly the meaning of the Catechism, and show how it all applies to the heart and life of every one. It is not at all the pastor's place, and it should never be expected of him, to act the school-master, to see to and oversee the memorizing of the answers. It is his office to expound and apply the truth, to make the doctrines clear to the minds of the learners, and to show how they are all related to the individual life.

But, alas, how little is this understood or practiced! How many parents, who call themselves Christians, and Lutherans, seem to think that they have nothing to do in this whole matter! They seem to think that if they send their children once a week, for a few months, to the pastor's class, they have done their whole duty. They do not even help and encourage the children to learn the lessons that the pastor assigns. And thus does this part of the pastor's work, which ought to be among the most delightful of all his duties, become wearisome. Scarcely anywhere else in all his duties does a pastor feel so hopeless and discouraged, as when standing week after week before a class of young people who have such poor instructors at home.

Christian parents, if you desire your sons and your daughters to become steadfast and useful members of the Church of Christ, see to it that you do your part in their religious instruction. Insist on it, and use your parental authority, if necessary, that your children learn the Catechism and regularly attend the pastor's instructions. We believe that the trouble in this matter lies largely in the fact that in many quarters catechization has become unpopular in our fast age. It is looked upon as a mark of old-fogyism, if not as an evidence of the absence of "spiritual religion!" The new measures and methods of modern revivals are more acceptable to the fickle multitude. They seem to point out a shorter route and quicker time to heaven. As a boy once said to the writer: "I don't want to belong to your church, because I would have to study the Catechism all winter, and down at the other church I can 'get through' in one night." That boy expressed about as clearly and tersely as could well be done, the popular sentiment of the day.

Yielding to this popular sentiment, many churches that once adhered strictly and firmly to the catechetical method, have either dropped it entirely or are gradually giving it up. And in order to clothe their spiritual ignorance and laziness in a pious garb, they say: "The Bible is enough for us." "We don't need any man-made Catechisms." "It is all wrong anyhow to place a human book on a level with or above the Bible." "We and our children want our religion from the Spirit of God, and not from a Church Catechism." Do such people know what they are talking about, or do they sometimes use these pious phrases to quiet a guilty conscience! Do they know what a Catechism is? Look at it for a moment. What is the nature and object of Luther's Small Catechism? Is it in the nature of a substitute for the Bible? Does it try to set aside the Bible? We hardly have enough patience to write such questions. No! No! Any child that can read this little book knows better. The plainest reader cannot fail to see that it is intended as a help to understand the Bible. Its purpose is to develop and awaken for the learner a more intelligent appreciation and love for the Bible. It contains nothing but Bible truth. Its design is simply this: To summarize and systematize the most important truths and doctrines of the divine Word: To so arrange and group them that even a child may learn what the Bible teaches as to creation, sin, salvation, and the means whereby it may be attained. We have the assurance, also—and we believe that history and observation will bear out the statement—that those who appreciate and have studied a sound scriptural Catechism most thoroughly, appreciate, understand, love and live their Bibles most sincerely.

10

The Small Catechism

Contents, Arrangement and Excellence of Luther's Small Catechism.

WE have spoken of Luther's Small Catechism as a help with which to lay hold of and to understand the most important truths of the Bible. These fundamental truths are taken from the Scriptures, and are so grouped, arranged and explained in the Catechism that the learner can easily grasp and understand them. That some of the truths contained in the Bible are of greater importance than others will hardly be denied. It is certainly more important that the child should know and understand the Ten Commandments, than that it should be familiar with all the details of the ceremonial law. Certainly better to be familiar with the Apostles' Creed, than to know all about the building of the Temple. Better be able to repeat and understand the Lord's Prayer, than to have a clear knowledge of the elaborate ritual of the Temple service. Better understand the meaning of Christ's two Sacraments than to be able to tell all about the great feasts of the Jews.

If anyone can know all these other matters also, so much the better. The Catechism will certainly be a help instead of a hindrance to this end. But if all cannot be learned —at least not at once—let the most important be taught first. And for this we have a Catechism. Look at its contents. It is divided into five parts. Each division treats of a separate subject. The first contains the Ten Commandments, with a brief and clear explanation of each Commandment. The second part has the three articles of the Apostles' Creed, with a clear and most beautiful explanation of each one. The third is the Lord's Prayer, its introduction, the seven petitions, and the conclusion; with a terse, though comprehensive explanation of each sentence. The fourth and fifth parts treat similarity of the two sacraments, Baptism and the Lord's Supper. Here then we have, in a brief space, the most important teachings of the important teachings of the whole Bible systematically arranged and clearly explained.

Of these contents and their arrangement, Luther himself says:

This Catechism is truly the Bible of the laity (or common people), wherein is contained the entire doctrine necessary to be known by every Christian for salvation. Here we have first the Ten Commandments of God, the doctrine of doctrines, by which the will, of God is known, what God would have us to do and what is wanting in us.

Secondly: The Apostles' Creed, the history of histories or the highest history, wherein are delivered to us the wonderful works of God from the beginning, how we and all creatures are created by God, how all are redeemed by the Son of God, how we are also received and sanctified by the Holy Ghost, and collected together to a people of God, and have the remission of sins and everlasting salvation. Thirdly: The Lord's Prayer, the prayer of prayers, the highest prayer which the highest Master taught, wherein are included all temporal and spiritual blessings, and comfort in trouble and in the hour of death.

Fourthly: The blessed Sacraments, the ceremonies of ceremonies, which God himself has instituted and ordained, and therein assured us of his grace.

The Catechism is a brief instruction in the Christian religion, and includes in itself the doctrine of the Law of God, Christian Faith, the Lord's Prayer, the institutions of Holy Baptism and of the Lord's Supper, which five parts are an epitome and kernel of the entire Holy Scriptures, for which reason it is called a 'Little Bible.'" Dr. Seiss, in his *Ecclesia Lutherana*, says:

It is the completest summary of the contents of the Bible ever given in the same number of words. It gave to the reviving Church a textbook for the presentation of the truth as it is in Jesus to the school, lecture-room and pulpit.

The sainted Dr. Krauth says:

The Catechism is a thread through the labyrinth of divine wonders. Persons often get confused, but if they will hold on to this Catechism it will lead them through without being lost. It is often called the 'Little Bible' and 'the Bible of the laity' because it presents the plain and simple doctrines of the Holy Book in its own words. Pearls strung are easily carried, unstrung they are easily lost. The Catechism is a string of Bible Pearls. The order of arrangement is the historical—the Law, Faith, Prayer, Sacrament of Baptism, and all crowned with the Lord's Supper—just as God worked them out and fixed them in history.

Thus we might go on quoting page after page of words of admiration and praise, from the greatest minds in our own and in other Churches, of the contents and arrangement of this little book. Neither can we charge these writers with extravagance in their utterances. For the more we examine and study the pages of this little book, the more we are convinced that it is unique and most admirable in its matter and plan. Let each one look for a moment into himself, and then from himself into this little book after this manner. I come into this world ignorant, yet full of presentiments and questions. I learn my first vague lesson about myself and God. I naturally ask: For what purpose has God put me here? What does He want me to do? The Catechism answers: To do His will, to keep His commandments. Here they are, and this is what they mean. I must have faith. I must believe. But what shall I believe? Answer: This summary of truth called the Apostles' Creed. It tells me of my Creator—His work and providence, and His gift of a Redeemer. It tells me of that Redeemer and His redemption; of the gift of the Spirit, and of His application of redemption. It not only tells me what to believe, but in the very telling it gives me power to believe. But I am still weak and more or less perplexed. Whither shall I go for more strength and Grace? My Catechism furnishes the answer: Go to the great Triune God. Ask Him in prayer. Here is a model. It will teach you how to pray. I learn what it is to pray. But again

I ask: How do I know that God will hear my prayer? Is He interested in me personally! Has He any other means besides His written Word to assure me of His love and to give me, in answer to my prayers, encouragement to believe Him and love Him? My Catechism points me to my baptism. It teaches me what it means, and how that in it I have God's own pledge that He is my Father who has renewed, reconciled and adopted me, and that I am truly His child. Here then is a fountain to which I can return again and again when weak and perplexed. Further, my Catechism teaches me concerning my Saviour's last legacy of love before His death for me, His Holy Supper. In it He holds out to me and gives to me, personally and individually, Himself and all His heavenly Grace. For my famishing soul this holy Sacrament is meat indeed and drink indeed.

Thus does this little Catechism meet me in my perplexity, take me by the hand, and lead me through the labyrinth of the wonders of Grace. It tells me what I am, what I need, and where and how to get what I need. It takes me to the wells of salvation. It draws from them living water. It holds it to my parched lips. It gathers the precious manna of the Word, and feeds me when I am faint and weary. Such is Luther's Small Catechism. Is it any wonder that we love it? Is it any wonder that we consider the study of it as part of The Way of Salvation in the Lutheran Church?[2]

---

[2] On the wisdom of the arrangement and sequence of Luther's Five Parts see The Lutheran Catechist, pp. 95-102.

11

Teaching the Catechism

Manner and Object of Teaching Luther's Catechism

WE have spoken of the importance of catechization. We have seen that Luther's Small Catechism is indeed a priceless Bible manual. It sets God's plan of salvation before us in matchless order. It is so full and yet so brief, so doctrinal and yet so warm and hearty. "The only Catechism," says Dr. Loehe, "that can be prayed." "It may be bought for sixpence," says Dr. Jonas, "but six thousand worlds could not pay for it." No wonder that no book outside of the Bible has been translated into so many languages, or circulated so widely. Thirty-seven years after its publication one hundred thousand copies were in circulation. The first book translated into any of the dialects of the American Indian, it was from its pages that the Native American read his first lessons concerning the true God, and his own relations to that God.

At the present day it is taught in a score of different languages in our own land.[3] And yet it is often neglected and abused, even by those who bear its author's name! It is neglected, if not entirely ignored, in countless Lutheran homes and Sunday-schools. It is even neglected by many so-called

---

[3] On the history of Luther's Small Catechism see The Lutheran Catechist

Lutheran pastors. They reject the testimony of four centuries. They set their own opinions above the testimony of the wisest, as well as the most deeply spiritual and consecrated witnesses of their own Church. They prefer the baseless, shallow, short-cut methods of this superficial age. Some of them have even joined in the cry of the fanatic, and called all catechization in the Church dead formalism! Fortunately, their number is growing rapidly less, and many, who for a while were carried away with the tide of new measures, are asking for and returning to the good and tried old ways.

Not only is this Catechism neglected, but it is and has been much abused. Abused, not only by its enemies, who have said hard things against it, but it has been and still is abused, like all good things, by its professed friends. And doubtless it is the abuse by its friends that is largely responsible for much of the neglect and contempt into which it sometimes has fallen. Thus in the family, it is still too often taught as a burdensome task. The home teacher often has no higher aim than that the children should learn it by rote—learn to rattle it off like the multiplication table, or the rules of grammar. Worse than this, it has often been used as an instrument of punishment. A child has done something wrong. It is angrily told that for this it must learn a page or two of the Catechism! The task is sullenly learned and sullenly recited; and the Catechism is hated worse than the sin committed. Then, too, it is slurred over in the Sunday-schools, without an earnest word of explanation or application.

The learner does not realize that it is meant to move the heart and to influence the life. This same sad mistake is also made by many pastors in the catechetical class. Strange as it may seem, this mistake is most commonly made by those very pastors who profess to be the few pastors who catechize their classes after the schoolmaster fashion. They go through the exercise in a perfunctory, formal manner. They insist on the letter of the text, and are satisfied if their pupils know the lessons well by rote! To urge on the dull and lazy pupil they will scold and rage, and even use the rod! The Catechism becomes a mere text-book. The pupils get out of it a certain amount of head knowledge. There are so many answers and so many proof texts that must be committed to memory. And when all this is well gotten and recited by rote, the teacher is satisfied, the pupil is praised, imagines that he has gotten all the good out of that book, and is glad that he is done with it!

Now we would not for a moment depreciate the memorizing of the Catechism. It is of the most vital importance, and cannot be too strongly urged. What we object to—and we cannot object too strenuously—is the idea that head knowledge is enough! Of course there must be head knowledge. The memory should store up all the precious pearls of God's truth that are found in the Catechism. The mind must grasp these truths and understand their meaning and their relation to one another. But if it stops here, it is not yet a knowledge that makes one wise unto salvation. In spiritual matters the enlightening or instructing of the intellect is not the end aimed at, but only a means to an end. The end aimed at must always be the renewal of the heart. The heart must be reached through the understanding. To know about Christ is not life eternal. I must know about Him before I can know Him. But I might know all about Him, be perfectly clear as to His person and His work, and stop there without ever knowing Him as heart only can know heart, as my personal Savior, my Lord and my God.

Here, we fear, many ministers make a sad mistake. They are too easily satisfied with a mere outward knowledge of the truth. They forget that even if it were possible to "understand all mystery and knowledge"—and not have "love" i.e. the love of God in Christ from a repentant heart, it would profit nothing. The true aim and end of all catechetical instruction in the Sunday-school, in the family, and especially in the pastor's class, should ever be a penitent, believing and loving heart in each catechumen.

We have, in a former chapter, shown the duty of the Sunday-school teacher in this matter. The pastor should likewise use all diligence to find out in who, among his catechumens, the germs of the divine life, implanted in baptism, have been kept alive, and in whom they are dormant. Where the divine life, given in holy baptism, has been fostered and cherished—where there has been an uninterrupted enjoyment of baptismal Grace, more or less clear and conscious—there it is the pastor's privilege to give clearer views of truth and Grace, to lead into a more intelligent and hearty fellowship with the Redeemer, to deepen penitence and to strengthen faith through the quickening truth of God's word.

Where, on the other hand, the seeds of baptismal Grace have been neglected, where the germs of the new life lie dormant or asleep, or where there never has been any implanting of Grace through Word or Sacrament—in short, where there are no pulsations, no manifestations of the new life, there the pastor has a different duty. He must endeavor to so bring the acquired truth to bear on the conscience and heart, as to awaken and bring about a sense of sin, a genuine sorrow therefor, a hatred thereof, a longing for deliverance, a turning to Christ and a laying hold on Him as the only help and the only hope.

Thus the one great aim and object of the conscientious pastor, with each impenitent catechumen, is to awaken and bring about genuine, heartfelt penitence and a true, trusting, clinging faith. In one word, he must labor for that catechumen's conversion. Only those of whom there is evidence that they are in a converted state should be to tell when, and where, and how he was converted. We mean simply this: That each one must have in his heart true penitence, i.e., sorrow for and hatred of sin, and true faith, i.e., a confiding, trustful embracing of Christ as the only Savior. Whether these elements of the new life have been constantly and uninterruptedly developed from Baptism, or whether they have been awakened gradually by the Word, is not material. The only important question is: Are the elements of the new life now there—even though as yet feeble and very imperfect—is the person now turned away from sin to a Savior? If so, we consider that person in a converted state. This much, we believe, should be demanded of each catechumen before he is admitted to the rite of confirmation.

It is largely because this has not been demanded as the only true and satisfactory result of catechization, that this important branch of the Church's activity has so largely been lost. It is doubtless because of carelessness on this point that so many fall back after confirmation to the world, the flesh and the devil. They did not hold fast to their crown because they had no crown. Where the Catechism is properly learned, understood and applied, the intellect is used as the gateway to the heart. Where the result of an enlightened mind is a changed heart, there are intelligent believers. They know what it means to be a Christian. They have an earnest desire for closer fellowship with Him who has loved them and washed them from their sins in His own blood. There is good hope that these will be faithful unto death.

12

Confirmation

IN our studies concerning the methods of Grace, or the application of the salvation purchased by Christ to the sinful race of Adam's children, we necessarily had to begin with the new-born child. We noted the first known operations of Grace at the baptismal font. We traced the infant through the holy influences received at a Christian mother's knee, and in the nurture of a Christian home. We followed up through the lessons and influences of the Church's nursery, the Sunday school, and from thence into the pastor's catechetical class. We have learned that these are the different successive steps in the Way of Salvation. This is God's way in the sanctuary. It begins at the baptismal font, where the child is received as a member of the Church of Christ; it leads through the Church in the house, and through the house keeps up a living connection with the Church. It is making disciples in accordance with Christ's plain directions, viz., "baptizing them, and teaching them." We have also admitted all along that there may be some who will go cast it away from the heart. This class we leave, for the present. We shall consider them further on.

We speak now of those who have been made disciples; who have not resisted the gracious influences of the Spirit of God, working through the sacramental and the written Word. Their minds are enlightened; they know something of sin and Grace and the bestowal and reception of Grace; they have an intelligent understanding of the plan of salvation revealed in the

Word of God. But this is not all. Their hearts also have been drawn ever nearer and closer to their dear Savior; they believe in and love the Lord Jesus Christ; they are ready to give an answer to every man that asks of them a reason of the hope that is in them. In the ardor and fervor of their young hearts' devotion they can repeat these beautiful words of their catechism and say:

I believe that Jesus Christ, true God, begotten of the Father from eternity, and also true man, born of the Virgin Mary, is my Lord; who has redeemed me, a lost and condemned creature, secured and delivered me from all sin, from death, and from the power of the devil . . . in order that I might be His, live under Him in His kingdom and serve Him in everlasting righteousness, innocence and blessedness.

Further, they can joyfully say:

I believe that I cannot by my own reason and strength believe in Jesus Christ my Lord, or come to Him. But that the Holy Ghost has called me through the Gospel, enlightened me by His gifts, sanctified and preserved me in the true faith.

This happy faith of their hearts has never been publicly professed before men. But the Word of God demands not only faith in the heart, but also confession by the lips.

If you confess with your mouth that Jesus is Lord and believe in your heart that God raised him from the dead, you will be saved. For with the heart one believes and is justified, and with the mouth one confesses and is saved (Romans 10:9-10).

Jesus also says, Matthew 10:32: "So everyone who acknowledges me before men, I also will acknowledge before my Father who is in heaven." If anyone is ashamed of this confession and refuses to make it, Jesus clearly says that of him He also will be ashamed in the judgment day. The Bible nowhere recognizes a secret discipleship. There are no promises to him who does not confess.

If our catechumens would therefore still follow God's Way of Salvation he must now also take this step, and publicly confess Jesus as his Lord and Redeemer and himself as His disciple. And for this there is no time so appropriate as when he desires to be numbered among the communicants of the congregation and participate with them in the celebration of the Lord's Supper. For this also our Church has made fitting arrangement. It is done at, or is rather a part of, the impressive ceremony of confirmation. Who has not witnessed this beautiful and touching rite? And what could be more interesting or impressive than to see a company of young hearts encircling the altar of Christ, confessing their faith, and bowing the knee to their Savior amid the prayers and benedictions of the Church? This is confirmation.

The catechumen has been examined by the pastor as to his fitness for this important step. The pastor has found that he possesses an intelligent understanding of the doctrines taught in the Catechism, and that the experience of his heart bears witness to their truth and power.[4] On this account he is seen as fit and well prepared to be admitted to the holy communion. He now comes of his own accord— not because he is old enough, or knows enough, or because father, mother, or pastor wants him to—before the altar of Christ. There, in the presence of the assembled congregation and the all-seeing God, his lips confess the faith of his heart, the faith into which he was baptized as a child. He now voluntarily takes upon himself the vows and promises that parents or sponsors took for him at baptism. He receives an earnest admonition from his pastor to hold fast that which he has and to be faithful unto death. The whole congregation, together with the pastor, lift their hearts in earnest intercessory prayer to God for His continuous blessing on and protection of the one in turn, by laying his hands on him and offering up for him a fervent petition in inspired words.

This is the simple and appropriate ceremony which we call confirmation. We claim for it no magical powers. It is not a sacrament. It adds nothing to the sacrament of baptism, for that is complete in itself. There is no conferring of Grace by the pastor's hands, but simply a directing of the Word and the Church's prayers to the individual. The confirming, strengthening and establishing of the catechumen in Grace, is effected primarily and alone

---

[4] On deciding as to who ought to be admitted to Confirmation see further The Lutheran Catechist, Chapter xvii.

through Christ's own means of Grace, viz.: the Word and the Sacraments. The Word has been applied to mind and heart all along from tender childhood. It is now brought home in the review and admonition of the pastor, amid specially solemn surroundings. The previous administering of baptism, and the perpetual efficacy of that sacrament, are now vividly recalled and impressed. And this unusually impressive application of the power of Word and Sacrament confirms and strengthens the divine life in the catechumen. Thus the means of Grace do the confirming, or rather the Holy Spirit through these means.

Instrumentally also the pastor may be said to confirm, since he, as Christ's ambassador or agent, applies His means of Grace. In still another, though inferior sense, the catechumen confirms. He receives the offered means of Grace, assents to their truth and efficacy, obtains divine virtue and strength through them, and with this imparted strength lays hold on Christ, draws nearer to Him, is united to Him as the branch to the vine, and thus confirms and establishes the covenant and bond that unites him to his Savior.

We do not claim for the rite of confirmation a "thus saith the Lord." We do not claim that it possesses sacramental efficacy, or that it is absolutely essential to salvation. We do claim, however, that there is nothing unevangelical or anti-scriptural in this ceremony. On the apostolic usage, we can find it in all its essential features in the pure age of the Church immediately succeeding the Apostles. In some form or other it has been practiced in the Church ever since. True, it has often been and is still grossly abused. It has often been encumbered and entangled with error and superstition; and therefore there have been some radical purists who have not only set it aside, but condemn it as Romish and heathen. The more sober and conservative churches have been content to get rid of its error and superstition. In its purified form they prize it highly, cherish its use, practice it, and find it attended by God's richest blessing.

It is a significant fact also that some of those who were once its most bitter opponents are gradually returning to its practice. We find, for example, that certain Presbyterian churches confirm large classes of catechumens every year. Certain Methodist book concerns and publishing houses also publish confirmation certificates, from which we infer that some of their churches also must practice this rite. Again, we find in certain "pastors' record books," gotten up to suit all denominations, columns for reporting the number of confirmations. All churches must indeed have some kind of a ceremony for the admission of the young into the communion of the church. And there certainly is no more befitting, beautiful and touching ceremony than confirmation, as described above and practiced in the Lutheran Church.

13

The Lord's Supper: Introduction

The Lord's Supper: Preliminary Observations

OUR catechumen has now been confirmed. The pastor has given him, in the name of the congregation, the right hand of fellowship, and also publicly authorized him to join with the congregation in the celebration of the Lord's Supper. For the first time, then, the young Christian is to partake of this holy sacrament, in order that he may be still further strengthened and confirmed in the true faith. This sacred institution is also a part of God's "Way of Salvation." It is one of the means of Grace appointed and ordained by Christ. It "has been instituted for the special comfort and strengthening of those who humbly confess their sins and who hunger and thirst after righteousness."

It is true that multitudes do not regard it as a means or channel of Grace. To them it is only an ancient rite or ceremony, having no special significance or blessing connected with it. If there is any blessing at all attached to it, it consists in the pious thoughts, the holy emotions and the sacred memories, which the communicant tries to bring to it and which are in some way deepened by it. At best, it is a memorial of an absent Savior, and in some form a representation of His sufferings and death. Now if this were all that we could see in the Lord's Supper, we would not regard it as a part of God's

Way of Salvation.

But our Church sees much more in it. With her it is indeed an essential and integral part of that Way. And since this is another point in which the Lutheran Church differs materially from many others, it would be good for us to devote some space and time to study it. A lot has been written on this important subject. We may not have anything new to add, but it is good to recall and re-study the old truths, which are so easily forgotten. Before we consider the nature of this sacrament, we make a few preliminary observations that will help us to guard against false views, and to arrive at correct conclusions.

We observe first, the importance of bearing in mind the source from which this institution has come. Who is its author? What is the nature or character of its origin? Our views of any institution are generally more or less influenced by thus considering its origin. Where did the Church get this ordinance which she has so conscientiously kept and devoutly celebrated? Did it come from the wisdom of man? Did some zealous mystic or hermit invent it, because forsooth he supposed it would be pleasant and profitable to have such an ordinance in the Church? Or did some early Church Council institute it, because those earnest fathers in their wisdom deemed it necessary that the Church should have such a service? Can it, in short, be traced to any human origin? If so, then we can deal with it as with any other human institution. We are then at liberty to reason and speculate about it. We can apply to it the rules of human science and learning. We can test it, measure it, sound it by philosophy, logic, and the laws of the mind. Each one then has a right to his own opinion about it. Each one can apply to it the test of common sense, and draw his own conclusion.

But this is not a human institution. The church has received it from the hands of the Son of God. It was ordained by Him who could say, "All power is given to Me in heaven and on earth,"(Matthew 28:17) and, "in him the whole fullness of deity dwells bodily" (Colossians 2:9) who, even before his birth in human form, was called "the Mighty God, the everlasting Father, the Prince of Peace"(Isaiah 9:6). When we come to deal with an institution of His, we dare never expect to fathom or test it by our poor, short-sighted and sin-blinded reason, philosophy, science, or common sense:

For my thoughts are not your thoughts neither are your ways my ways, declares the LORD. For as the heavens are higher than the earth, so are my ways higher than your ways and my thoughts than your thoughts (Isaiah 55:8-9).

Whenever, therefore, we come to deal with anything that comes from His hands, it is no longer of the earth and is not subject to earthly laws and human rules. His acts, His deeds, His words, belong to the realm of faith, and not of reason. Reason must ever be taken captive and made to bow before the heavenly things connected with Him. Or shall we try to reason out His human birth, His growth, His nature, His deeds? Shall we reason out the feeding of the multitudes with those few barley loaves and fishes? No; they came through His hands, and the power of those hands we cannot comprehend. We cannot comprehend how that afflicted woman could receive virtue, health and life, by touching the hem of His garment—a mere fabric of cloth—or how the clay and spittle from His hands could open the eyes of one born blind. Whenever, therefore, we come to study this ordinance, let us ever bear in mind its divine origin. It is the Lord's Supper. This precaution will be a safeguard against error, and a help to the truth.

We notice secondly the time of institution. It was "in the night in which He was betrayed." That awful night, when the clouds of divine wrath were gathered over Him, and were ready to burst upon Him; when the accumulated guilt of a sinful race was all to be laid on Him, borne by Him as though it were His own, and its punishment endured as though He had committed every sin. Then, when the strokes of justice were about to fall, our blessed Savior, gathered his small band of disciples before His crucifixion. He spoke to them His farewell words, uttered His high-priestly prayer, instituted and administered to them this holy sacrament. All the surroundings conspired to throw round it a halo of heavenly mystery. Everything was calculated to impress that little band that what He now ordained and made binding on the Church, till He would come again, was something more than an empty sign or ceremony. Thus the time, the circumstances, and all the surroundings of the institution of this holy sacrament, prepare us in advance to believe that there must be in it or connected with it some heavenly gift of Grace that can be obtained nowhere else.

We notice thirdly the significant term by which Jesus designates this institution. When he administered the cup He said: "This cup is the New Testament in my blood." He calls it a testament. A testament is a last will. Jesus was about to go forth to die. Before he departed, He made His will. He gives the Church an inheritance. The legacy that He leaves is this sacrament. Before we undertake to study the words of the institution, we wish to impress this thought. A will is the last place where one would use ambiguous or figurative language. Every maker or writer of a will strives to use the clearest and plainest words possible. Every precaution is taken that there may be no doubtful or difficult expression employed. The aim of the maker is to make it so plain that only one meaning can be taken from it. Neither is any one permitted to read into it any sense different from the clear, plain, literal meaning of the words. Fanciful, metaphorical, or far-fetched interpretations are never applied to the words of a will. Much less is any one permitted to change the words by inserting or substituting other words than those used by the maker. Christ's words of institution are the words of His last Will and Testament.

14

The Lord's Supper (Part 2)

The Lord's Supper Continued

IN the former chapter we made some preliminary observations, intended to be helpful, as guards against false conclusions, and as guides to a correct understanding of the subject under consideration. It is important that we always keep these in mind in our study of the doctrine of the Lord's Supper. Let us always keep before us, therefore, the Author or Founder of this institution, the time and circumstances of the institution, and its testamentary character. We are now ready to inquire further into the nature and meaning of this holy ordinance. And in order to determine this we desire to go directly to the law and to the testimony. We want to know, first of all: what does the Word of God teach on the subject?

Before we proceed, however, to note and examine the passages of Scripture that discuss the issue, let's recall what we said about the interpretation of Scripture in one of the chapters on the Sacrament of Baptism. We stated there that our Church has certain plain and safe principles of interpretation that are to guide those who are studying God's Word:

1. A passage is to be taken in its plain, natural and literal sense, unless there is something in the text itself, or in the context, that clearly indicates

that it is meant to be figurative.
2. A passage is never to be torn from its context, but it is to be studied in connection with what goes before and what follows after.
3. Scripture is to be interpreted by Scripture, the obscure passages are to be compared with the more clear, bearing on the same subject.
4. We can never be fully certain that a doctrine is Scriptural until we have examined and compared all that the Word says on the subject.

On these principles we wish to examine what the Word teaches as to the nature of the Sacrament of the Lord's Supper. We note first the accounts of the institution as given by the three Evangelists, Matthew, Mark, and Luke. In Matthew 26:26-28, we read:

Now as they were eating, Jesus took bread, and after blessing it broke it and gave it to the disciples, and said, "Take, eat; this is my body." And he took a cup, and when he had given thanks he gave it to them, saying, "Drink of it, all of you, for this is my blood of the covenant, which is poured out for many for the forgiveness of sins.

With this the accounts in Mark 15:22-24, and in Luke 22:19-20, substantially agree. There is a slight variation of the words, but the substance is the same. We notice only this difference: Luke adds the words, "Do this in remembrance of Me." On this point let's notice, in passing, that St. Luke's was the last written of the three. The Gospels of Matthew and Mark had been written and were read and used in the church several years before St. Luke's. And yet the two former do not contain the words, "Do this in remembrance of Me." Now we submit right here, if to remember Christ were all that is in this sacrament, or even the primary thing, why did those who were inspired to write the first Gospels, and knew that there were no others, leave out these words? Almost thirty years after the time of the institution of the sacrament, the great Apostle wrote a letter to the Church at Corinth. That Church was made up of a mixed multitude—Jews and Gentiles, freemen and slaves. Many of them were neither clear nor sound on points of Christian doctrine and practice. In his fatherly and affectionate letters to the members of this Church, Paul, among other things, gives them instruction concerning this sacrament; and, lest some of them might perhaps suppose that he is giving them merely his own wisdom and speculation, he takes especial care to disavow this:

For I received from the Lord what I also delivered to you, that the Lord Jesus on the night when he was betrayed took bread, and when he had given thanks, he broke it, and said, "This is my body which is for you. Do this in remembrance of me." In the same way also he took the cup, after supper, saying, "This cup is the new covenant in my blood. Do this, as often as you drink it, in remembrance of me (1 Corinthians 11:23-25).

He gives in substance the same words of institution as given by the Evangelists. After giving them the words of institution, Paul goes on to instruct them about worthy and unworthy communing. In these instructions we cannot help but notice how he takes the real presence of Christ's body and blood for granted all the way through. Notice his language in verse 27:

Whoever, therefore, eats the bread or drinks the cup of the Lord in an unworthy manner will be guilty concerning the body and blood of the Lord.

And verse 29:

For anyone who eats and drinks without discerning the body eats and drinks judgment on himself.

Going back to chapter ten, verse sixteen, we find the Apostle giving the doctrine of the Lord's Supper in a few words thus:

The cup of blessing that we bless, is it not a participation in the blood of Christ? The bread that we break, is it not a participation in the body of Christ?

We have now noted all the passages that speak directly on this subject. There are other strong passages that are often quoted in defense of the doctrine of the real presence, and which we doubtless have a right to use in corroboration of those above quoted. We refer to John 6:53-56:

So Jesus said to them, "Truly, truly, I say to you, unless you eat the flesh of the Son of Man and drink his blood, you have no life in you. Whoever feeds on my flesh and drinks my blood has eternal life, and I will raise him up on the last day. For my flesh is true food, and my blood is true drink. Whoever feeds on my flesh and drinks my blood abides in me, and I in him.

THE LORD'S SUPPER (PART 2)

As to the disputed point, whether this refers to the Lord's Supper or not, we are willing to waive it here. We are content to take those passages quoted above, which everyone acknowledges as referring directly to our subject. These we would have the reader carefully examine. Note particularly the language, the words employed. In the four accounts given of the institution, three by the Evangelists and one by Paul, we have the same clear, plain words concerning the bread and wine—words of the last will and testament of the Son of God our Savior— "This is my body;" "This is my blood of the New Testament;" or "the New Testament in my blood." Note the language of Paul: "Guilty of the body and blood of the Lord." "Not discerning the Lord's body." The cup is called the communion of the blood, and the bread, the communion of the body of Christ. The word communion is made up of two Latin words, *con* and *unio*, meaning union with, or connection with. The marginal reading in our family Bibles, as well as in the revised version, is "participation in." The plain English of the verse then is, the bread is a participation in, or a connection with Christ's body, and the wine with His blood. We are now ready to take all these passages together, to compare them one with another, and to ask, What do they teach? What is the Bible doctrine of the Lord's Supper? Is it transubstantiation? Is it consubstantiation? Is it that the bread and wine are mere representations or memorials of the absent body and blood of Christ? Or do these passages teach "That the body and blood of Christ are truly present under the form of bread and wine and are communicated to those that eat in the Lord's Supper?" (Augsburg Confession, Art. X).

15

The Lord's Supper (Part 3)

The Lord's Supper Concluded

WE have quoted, noted, collected and compared the words of Scripture that speak of the sacrament of the Lord's Supper. We now wish to ask and examine the question: What do these passages taken together and compared with one another teach? Or, in other words, what is the Bible doctrine of the Lord's Supper? Does the Bible teach the doctrine of Transubstantiation, as held and confessed by the Roman Catholic Church? If our investigation of the teachings of the Holy Scriptures convinces us that they teach Transubstantiation, we will be ready to believe and confess that doctrine, no matter who else may believe or disbelieve it. What we want to know, believe, teach and confess is Biblical doctrine. What is Transubstantiation? The word means a change of substance. The doctrine of the Roman Church is that after the consecration by the priest, the bread in the sacrament is changed into the material body of Christ, and the wine into His blood—so entirely changed that bread no longer remains, but only Christ's body, and that the wine no longer remains but has been converted into His blood. Is this the doctrine of God's word? Does the Word anywhere tell us that the bread and wine are changed in this way? Does it call the bread flesh, either before or after the consecration? Let us see. "Jesus took bread." "I will not drink of the fruit of the vine." "The bread which we break." "For as often as ye eat this bread and drink this cup." Such is the language of inspiration. Now we ask, if the Holy Spirit desired that plain and unprejudiced readers should find the doctrine of Transubstantiation in His words, why does He call the earthly elements bread and wine before, during and after the consecration and distribution? Why does He not say, "as often as ye eat this flesh and drink this blood?" Evidently because the bread is, and remains plain, natural bread, and so with the wine. There is no change in the component elements, in the nature, matter, or substance of either. Transubstantiation is not the doctrine of God's word; neither was it the doctrine of the early Church. It is one of the human inventions and corruptions of the Church of Rome. Do then these words of Scripture teach the doctrine of Consubstantiation? There are people who talk a great deal about Consubstantiation, and yet they do not know what it means. What is it? It is a mingling or fusing together of two different elements or substances, so that the two combine into a third. A familiar example, often given, is the fusing or melting together of copper and zinc until they unite and form brass. Applied to the sacrament of the altar, the doctrine of Consubstantiation would teach that the flesh and blood of Christ are physically or materially mingled and combined with the bread and wine, so that what the communicant receives is neither plain, real bread, nor real flesh, but a gross mixture of the two. Again we ask, is this the teaching of the Word? The very same proofs that convince us that the divine Word does not teach Transubstantiation, also convince us that it does not teach Consubstantiation. The simple fact that the earthly elements are called bread and the fruit of the vine, before, during and after consecration and distribution satisfies us that they remain plain, and do not become a different substance. Consubstantiation is not, nor has it ever been, the teaching of the Lutheran Church. It often has been, and is still called the Lutheran doctrine of the Lord's Supper, but it is found in none of her confessions. It was never taught by a single recognized theologian of our Church. One and all, they have repudiated it and repudiate it still.

The question then is still unanswered: What is the doctrine of the divine Word? There are many who have a ready and easy answer as to this doctrine.

They say it is only a Church ceremony, one of the old, solemn rites by which Church members are distinguished from outsiders. There is indeed no special significance or Grace connected with it. There is really nothing in it but bread and wine. There is no presence of Christ at all in this sacrament in any way different from His general presence. The bread represents or signifies, is a sign, or symbol, or emblem of Christ's body, and the wine of His blood. The communicant receives nothing but bread and wine, and while he partakes of these he remembers Christ's sufferings and death. Whatever special benefit he is to derive from this sacrament he must first put into it, by bringing to it pious thoughts, good feelings, deep emotions, tender memories, and a faith that swings itself aloft and holds communion with Christ far off in heaven. This is about the current, popular view of this subject as held and taught in nearly all the Protestant Churches of to-day, outside of the Lutheran Church.

As a natural consequence of this superficial view, the whole matter is treated very lightly. There is little, if any, solemn, searching preparation. In many places there is no formal consecration of the elements. The table is thrown open to anyone who desires to commune. There are no regulations, no guards, no disciplinary tests, connected with it. Even unbaptized people, and those who have never made a public profession of faith, are often permitted to commune. "We return to the question: Is the view just noticed in harmony with and based on the Word? Let us see. If there is nothing present but bread and wine, why does Christ say, "This is My body, My blood?" Why not say, "This is bread, this is wine." If Jesus wanted us to believe that these were merely symbols, why did He not say so? Did He not know how to use language? Did He use dark or misleading words in His last Will and Testament? Why does Paul, in speaking of worthy and unworthy communing, speak of the body of Christ as present, as a matter of course? Was he inspired to misunderstand Christ and lead plain readers astray? If there is nothing more in the sacrament than to remember Christ, why—as already noticed—did not the writers of the first two Gospels put in the words, "Do this in remembrance of Me?" Or why did not Christ plainly say," Take, eat this bread, which represents My body, in remembrance of Me?"

Clearly, the doctrine in question is not based on the words of Scripture.

It cannot be supported by Scripture. Neither do its defenders attempt to support it by the passages that clearly speak of this sacrament. If they try to bring in any Scripture proof, they quote passages that have nothing to do with the subject. They draw their proofs and supports principally from reason and philosophy. Surely a doctrine that changes the words of the institution, wrests and twists them out of their natural sense, and does violence to all sound rules of interpretation; that must bolster itself up by the very same methods of interpretation that are used to disprove the divinity of Christ, the resurrection of the body, and the eternity of future punishment, is not the doctrine of Christ. We have not found the Bible doctrine in any of the views examined. Can we find it? Let us see. We are satisfied, from our examination of the passages that have to do with our subject, that there must be earthly elements present in this sacrament. They are bread and wine. They remain so, without physical change or admixture. We also find from these passages that there is a real presence of heavenly elements. These are the body and blood of Christ. Not indeed that body as it was in its state of humiliation, when it was subject to weakness, hunger, thirst, pain and death. But that glorified, spiritual, resurrection body, in its state of exaltation, inseparably joined with the Godhead, and by it rendered everywhere present. And this body and divinity, we remark in it on the Mount of Transfiguration. It is of this body, and blood, of which Peter says, 1 Peter 1:18-19, that it is not a corruptible thing, and of which the Apostle says, Heb. 9:12, "By his own blood he entered in once into the Holy Place" (that is, into heaven), and of which Jesus spoke when He said, "Take eat, this is my body . . . this is my blood." Of this body and blood, the Scriptures affirm that they are present in the sacrament. The passage which sets forth the double presence, that of the earthly and heavenly elements, which indeed sums up and states the Bible doctrine in a few words, is 1 Corinthians 10:16:

The cup of blessing that we bless, is it not a participation in the blood of Christ? The bread that we break, is it not a participation in the body of Christ?

Here Paul affirms that the bread is the communion of Christ's body, not of His Spirit or His influence. If the bread is the communion of, participation in, or connection with His body, then bread and body must both be present. It takes two things to make a communion. They must both be present. It would be absurd to speak of bread as a communion of something in no way connected with it. As we have already said, the plain sense of the words of this passage is, that the bread is a connection with, or a participation in Christ's body, and so with the wine; so much so that whoever partakes of the one must, in some manner, also become a partaker of the other. The bread, therefore, becomes the medium, the vehicle, the conveyance, that carries to the communicant the body of Christ, and the wine likewise His blood. And this, we repeat, without any gross material transmutation or mixing together. The bread and wine are the earthly vessels that carry the Heavenly treasures of Christ's body and blood, even as the letters and words of the Scriptures convey to the reader or hearer the Holy Spirit. This is the clear, plain, Bible doctrine of the Lord's Supper. There is nothing gross, carnal, Capernaitish or repulsive about it. And exactly this is the teaching and doctrine of the Evangelical Lutheran Church. Article X., Augsburg Confession, says:

Of the Lord's Supper they teach that the true body and blood of Christ are truly present, under the form of bread and wine, and are there and blood of Jesus Christ, under the bread and wine, given unto us Christians to eat and drink, as it was instituted by Christ himself.

We therefore find that on this point also our dear old Church is built impregnably on the foundation of Christ and His Apostles. And though she may here differ from all others, she cannot yield one jot or tittle without proving false to her Lord and to His truth. It is not bigotry. It is not prejudice that makes her cling so tenaciously to this doctrine. She knows, as the great Reformer knew, that the very foundations are at stake; that if she gives up on this point, and changes the Scriptures to suit human reason, she will soon have to give up other doctrines, and by and by the rock on which the Church is built will be removed, and the gates of hell will prevail. And further, if there is any risk of being mistaken—which she, however, does not admit— she would rather run that risk, by taking her Master at His Word, than by changing His Word. In childlike confidence and trust, she would rather believe too much than too little. She would rather trust her dear Master too far than not far enough. And therefore here she stands; she cannot do otherwise. May God help her! Amen. Others may still say, "This is a hard saying, who can bear it? The idea of eating and drinking the body and blood of our Lord offends us." Well, it also offends all rationalistic liberals, that their salvation should depend on the literal shedding of the literal blood of Jesus. But it does not offend us. On the contrary, this same doctrine is to us the very heart of the whole Gospel, and is therefore more precious than life itself. Neither does it offend us that the mother, whose pure and tender love to her infant child is an emblem of the divine love to us poor sinners, while she presses to her bosom that little one, soothes away its frettings and sings away its sobbings, at the same time feeds and nourishes that feeble life with her own physical life, giving it literally her body and blood. This is no offense to us. And why should it offend us that our dear loving Savior comes so of the yearning love of His divine heart, and, at the same time, feeds us with His own spiritual and glorified body and blood, and thus makes us partake of the divine nature. Instead of being offended, let us rather bow down, and worship, and adore, and sing:

Lord, at Thy table I behold
The wonders of Thy Grace;
But most of all admire that
I Should find a welcome place.
I that am all defiled by sin;
A rebel to my God:
I that have crucified His Son
And trampled on His blood!
What strange surprising Grace is this
That such a soul has room;
My Savior takes me by the hand,
And kindly bids me come!

16

The Confessional Service

The Preparatory Service; Sometimes Called the Confessional Service.

IN our examination of the nature and meaning of the Lord's Supper, we have found that it is indeed a most important and holy Sacrament. It is in fact the most sacred of all the ordinances of the Church on earth. There is nothing beyond it—nothing so heavenly, on this side of heaven, as this Feast. Nowhere else does the believer approach so near to heaven as when he stands or kneels, as a communicant at this altar, the Holy of Holies in the Church of Christ. What a solemn act! To approach this altar, to participate in its heavenly mysteries, to become a partaker of the glorified body and blood of the Son of God! Surely no one who understands the import of this Sacrament, will dare to approach hastily, thoughtlessly, or on the impulse of the moment. Surely there must be forethought and preparation. Our Church has realized this from the very beginning. She has had and still has a special service for those who intend to commune. Her preparatory service precedes the communion service. And we can safely affirm, that no Church has so searching and suitable a preparatory service as has the Lutheran Church. Where this preparatory service is properly conducted and entered into by pastor and people, it is an important step in the Way of Salvation. Our

Church, in this particular also, is purely scriptural. Israel of old had seasons of special preparation, previous to special manifestations from God. There was a season of special preparation before the giving of the Law; also before the receiving of the quails and the manna from heaven. There were days of preparation before and in connection with the great annual festivals, as well as in connection with other great national and religious events. Our Lord, Himself, observed a most solemn preparatory service with His disciples before He instituted the Last Supper. He not only spoke very comforting words to them, but He also plainly pointed out to them their sins, e. g., their pride, their jealousy, their quarrels, their coming defection, the fall of Peter and the treachery of Judas. In line with all this, Paul directs: "But let a person examine himself then, and so eat of the bread and drink of the cup"(1 Corinthians 11:28). And we have our preparatory service to assist the communicant in this examination. Its object is to enable the communicant to realize his own sinfulness, to deepen in him true penitence and longing for forgiveness, and also to aid him in appropriating and rejoicing in the full and free forgiveness of Christ. To this end we sing our penitential hymns, plead for Grace to know ourselves, our sinfulness, and the fullness of Christ's Grace, and hear such searching appeals from the pastor as often pain and agonize the heart. Then follows, on part of the congregation, a united audible and public confession of sin, and of an earnest desire for forgiveness, of faith in Christ as the divine Savior, and of an earnest purpose to hate and avoid all sin in the future. After this public confession in the presence of the pastor and of one another, the same confession is repeated, on bended knees, directly to God. This two-fold confession—first in the presence of the pastor and of one another, and then directly to God—is followed by the words of absolution from the pastor. In pronouncing the absolution the minister uses the following, or words to the same effect:

Almighty God, our heavenly Father, having of His great mercy promised the forgiveness of sins to all those who with hearty repentance and true faith turn unto Him, and having authorized His ministers to declare the same, I pronounce, to all who do truly repent and believe on the Lord Jesus Christ, and are sincerely determined to amend their ways and lead a godly and pious life, the entire forgiveness of all your sins, in the name of the Father, and of the Son, and of the Holy Ghost. Amen.

Then follow a few words in which he assures the impenitent and hypocritical that their sins are not forgiven, but will certainly bring upon them the fearful wrath of Almighty God, unless they speedily repent, turn from their sins, and fly to the Lord Jesus Christ for refuge and salvation. This is the closing part of the preparatory service, which is called Confession and Absolution. Some time ago we were asked, by a minister of another denomination, why Lutherans retained and practiced Romish confession, and forgiveness by the minister. We handed him our formula for Confession and Absolution, and asked him to examine it and point out to us wherein it was Romish or unscriptural. After examination he handed it back, saying: "I cannot say that it is exactly unscriptural. In fact, I can easily see how you can quote Scripture in its defense." Our Lord tells Peter "I will give you the keys of the kingdom of heaven, and whatever you bind on earth shall be bound in heaven, and whatever you loose on earth shall be loosed in heaven"(Matthew 16:19). In Matthew 18:18, the Savior gives the same power in the same words to all the disciples as representatives of the Christian congregation. In John 20:21-23, He says again to the disciples:

Jesus said to them again, "Peace be with you. As the Father has sent me, even so I am sending you." And when he had said this, he breathed on them and said to them, "Receive the Holy Spirit. If you forgive the sins of any, they are forgiven them; if you withhold forgiveness from any, it is withheld.

What do these words of Christ mean? They must mean something. They must be of some use. Our Lord certainly does confer some kind of authority or power on His Church, which is His Bride. Does He hereby give into her hand the keys of His kingdom, and authorize her to dispense its treasures? Does she through her ministry, employ these keys, bring forth heavenly treasures, and distribute and withhold them among the children of men? To the Church's ministers Christ says, Luke 10:16; "He that hears you, hears me; and the one who rejects you rejects me." One of these ministers, who certainly understood his office and its perogatives, speaking in the name of all true ministers of Christ, says, 2 Corinthians 5:20: "Therefore, we are ambassadors for Christ, God making his appeal through us. We implore you on behalf of Christ, be reconciled to God." If we would see how this ambassador exercised his high authority in an individual case, he tells us in 2 Corinthians 2:10: "Anyone whom you forgive, I also forgive. Indeed, what I have forgiven, if I have forgiven anything, has been for your sake in the presence of Christ." If now we take these passages together, we must admit that in their plain literal sense, they do teach that Christ, the Head of the Church, has in some sense committed to His Church the power to remit and retain sins, and that this power is exercised in the Church through its ministry. In what sense then does the minister have such authority? It can't be by virtue of himself or of a power originating in his own person. In this sense only God can forgive sin, as all sin is committed against Him. But God can delegate that power to another, and permit him to use it in His name. And this is all the power any human being can have in this matter. It would indeed be blasphemy for any man to claim that he had power in himself to forgive sins. If he can have any power at all, it must be Christ's power. He can only use it as a deputy, as an ambassador, or as an agent. And this is exactly what the Word teaches. The minister is Christ's ambassador. He beseeches and speaks in Christ's stead, as though God were speaking by him. Paul forgave the penitent Corinthian, not in his own name or by his own authority, but "in the person of Christ." When a part of our country was in rebellion, the government at Washington sent deputies to those who had renounced their allegiance, empowered to confer pardon, and reinstate as citizens, all who accepted the government's terms of pardon. These agents had no power in themselves, but they were authorized to carry the pardoning power of the government, and to those who accepted it from them, it was as valid as though each one had received a special proclamation of pardon from the government. Just so does the pastor, as Christ's ambassador, offer and bestow Christ's forgiveness to the penitent and believing sinner. He offers this pardon only on the terms laid down by Christ. The means through which he conveys this pardon is God's Word. This Word, preaching repentance and remission of sins, when spoken by the minister, is just as effective as when it fell from the lips of Christ or His inspired apostles. Whenever he preaches God's Word he does nothing else than declare Christ's absolution. It is the Word of God, that still remits and retains, that binds and looses. The pastor can only declare that Word, but the Word itself does effectually work forgiveness to him and rightly receives it. Not only does the Pastor carry this Word of God, this kingdom, this power of God unto salvation, and apply it, but any disciple of Christ can do so.

Dr. Krauth beautifully says: "The whole pastoral work is indeed but an extension of the Lutheran idea of Confession and Absolution." And Dr. Walther says: "The whole Gospel is nothing but a proclamation of the forgiveness of sins, or a publication of the same Word to all men on earth, which God Himself confirms in heaven." Dr. Seiss somewhere says: "Every time a believer in Christ sits down beside a troubled and penitent one, and speaks to such an one Christ's precious promises and assurances of forgiveness, he carries out the Lutheran or scriptural idea of absolution." And even the minister of another denomination, above referred to, acknowledged to the writer, that when he found one of his parishioners of whom he was convinced that she was a true penitent, despondent on account of her sins, he unhesitatingly said to her, "Your sins are forgiven by Christ." We had intended to still say something about the public confession of Israel at Mizpeh, 1 Samuel 5:6, and of the multitudes who went out to John the Baptist, Matt. 8:6; also of the private Confession and Absolution of David and Nathan, 2 Samuel 12:13. But each one can examine these cases for himself. Enough has been said to assure us that our Church, in this matter also, is grounded on the eternal Word of God, and that she did wisely when, after repudiating the blasphemous practices of the Roman confessional, she yet retained an evangelical Confession and Absolution. When we therefore hear the declaration of absolution from God's Word, let us believe it, "even as if it were a voice sounding from heaven." Therefore the Augsburg Confession, Article XXV, says that: "On account of the very great benefit of Absolution, as well as for other uses to the conscience, Confession is retained among us."

Such evangelical Confession and Absolution establishes and maintains the true relation that should exist between an evangelical pastor and the members of his flock. Instead of a mere preacher, a platform orator, he becomes a true spiritual guide, a curate for the cure of souls. He encourages his members to reveal to him their weaknesses, their besetting sins, their doubts and spiritual conflicts, in order that he may instruct, direct, comfort and strengthen them with the all-sufficient and powerful Word of God. And thus, wherever he finds true penitence and faith, however weak, he carries out the divine commission which directs him:

Comfort, comfort my people, says your God. Speak tenderly to Jerusalem, and cry to her that her warfare is ended, that her iniquity is pardoned, that she has received from the LORD's hand double for all her sins (Isaiah 40:1-2).

17

The Word as a Means of Grace

IN the last chapter we learned that the Word of God is the key of the kingdom, which key Christ has given to His Church, and that this Word, declared by the pastor, does really convey and apply the forgiveness of sins to the penitent and believing. Following out this idea, we wish to show now that God's Word is the power and the effective means through which the Holy Spirit operates on the minds and hearts of the children of men. The popular idea in regard to the use of the Word, seems to be that it is intended to be merely a book of instruction and a guide—that its purpose is merely to tell us about sin and salvation; that like a guide-post it points out the way of salvation, and shows the necessity of repentance, faith, and holiness. That it tells about the need of the Holy Spirit to effect a change of heart, and that further than this it affords no help for fallen man. A poor sinner goes to that Word. He reads it, or hears it preached. He learns indeed that he is a sinner, but he has no deliverance from sin. He learns of Christ's redemption, but its benefits aren't applied to him. He sees that he needs to repent and believe, but by his own strength he cannot. He learns further that he needs the Holy Spirit to enable him to repent and believe, but according to the current opinion, that Spirit is not in the Word, nor effective through it, but operates independently of it. The using of the divine Word is at best an occasion that the Spirit may use for independent operation. He might go from his Bible and from many a sermon and say: "I know I need religion—I need the Spirit of God, and I hope that at some time the Spirit may come to me and bless me with pardon and peace, but I cannot tell when or how this may be." According to this popular conception, the Holy Spirit might be compared to a dove flying about, and alighting at hap-hazard now on this one and then on that one. The Lutheran Church does not teach in this manner but claims that the Word does what it says. According to her faith the Word of God is more than a book of information. It not only tells about sin and salvation, but de livers from sin and confers salvation. It not only points out the way of life, but it leads, nay more, we might say, it carries us into and along that way. It not only instructs concerning the need of the Holy Spirit, but it conveys that Spirit to the very mind and heart. It is indeed a precious truth, that this Word not only tells me what I must do to be saved, but it also enables me to do it. It is indeed the principal means of Grace. It is the vehicle and instrument of the Holy Spirit. Through it the Holy Spirit works repentance and faith. Through it He regenerates, converts, and sanctifies. This is the doctrine of the Lutheran Church, concerning the use and efficacy of the divine Word. Luther's Small Catechism, Apostles' Creed, Article 3 explanation says:

I believe that I cannot by my own reason or strength believe in Jesus Christ my Lord, or come to Him; but that the Holy Spirit hath called me through the Gospel, enlightened me by His gifts,

Augsburg Confession, Article 5 also says:

For by the Word and Sacraments, as by instruments, the Holy Spirit is given; who works faith, where and when it pleases God, in those that hear the Gospel

This is the teaching of the Word itself also. John writes,

It is the Spirit who gives life; the flesh is no help at all. The words that I have spoken to you are spirit and life (John 6:63).

In Romans 1:16, Paul says of the Gospel:

It is the power of God unto salvation for everyone who believes.

For the word of God is living and active, sharper than any two-edged sword, piercing to the division of soul and of spirit, of joints and of marrow, and discerning the thoughts and intentions of the heart (Hebrews 4:12).

Since you have been born again, not of perishable seed but of imperishable, through the living and abiding word of God (1 Peter 1:23).

Therefore put away all filthiness and rampant wickedness and receive with meekness the implanted word, which is able to save your souls (James 1:21).

It is clear, therefore, that the Word does claim for itself virtue, life, power, and effectiveness. But does it claim to be the Spirit's means and instrument, by and through which He operates? In 2 Corinthians 3:8, it is called a "ministration of the Spirit." In Ephesians 6:17, Paul calls it the "sword of the Spirit." We learn the same truth from the fact that the same effects are ascribed indiscriminately to the Spirit and to the Word, showing clearly that where one is, there the other is also, and that one acts through the other. Thus the divine call is ascribed in one place to the Spirit and in another to the Word. Revelation 22:17. "The Spirit . . . says come." In the parables, Christ's ministers, preaching the Word, say: "Come, for all things are ready." In like manner, enlightening, or teaching, is ascribed to both. John 14:26, Jesus says of the Spirit: "He shall teach you all things;" chapter 16:13, "He shall guide you into all truth." He is called a "spirit of wisdom"—a "spirit of light." On the other hand, the Word is called a "Word of wisdom;" also, Psalm 119:130: "The entrance of your Word gives light;" 2 Timothy 3:15: The Scriptures are said to be "able to make wise unto salvation;" 2 Peter 1:19: It is as "a light that shines in a dark place."

So, also, regeneration is ascribed to both. John 3:5: "Born of water and the Spirit;" verse 6: "That which is born of the Spirit is spirit;" verse 8: "So is every one that is born of the Spirit;" 1 John 5:4: "For whoever is born of God (i. e., of God's Spirit) overcomes the world." But of the divine Word it is said, 1 Peter 1:17: "Born again by the living and abiding word of God." And James 1:18, "Of his own will he brought us forth by the word of truth." The work of sanctification is also ascribed to the Word and the Spirit. Jesus says, "Sanctify them in the truth; your word is truth;" but 1 Corinthians 6:11 calls it a work of the Spirit, "You are sanctified . . . by the Spirit of our God." And thus we might go on, and show that what is ascribed in one place to the Spirit, is ascribed in another place to the Word—proving conclusively that the two always go together. Where one is, there the other is also. The Spirit operates through the Word, whether it is the written, the preached, the sacramental, or the Word in conversation or reflection. The ordinary operations of the Holy Spirit are through that Word. Those who are renewed and sanctified by the Holy Spirit are those who have been influenced by this regenerating and sanctifying Word. This blessed Word of God, quick, powerful, able to save the soul, because of the life-giving Spirit connected with it, is not only to be read, but to be preached and heard. This is God's own arrangement. From the days of Enoch, Noah, the patriarchs and prophets, down to Jesus and the apostles, and from them to the end of the Gospel dispensation, He has had and will have His preachers of righteousness. Our Lord preached His own Gospel, the words of spirit and of life. He commissioned His apostles to preach the same Gospel. They "went out and preached everywhere"(Mark 16:20). The Church called and sent others, whose life-work it was to "preach the word, be ready in season and out of season, reprove, rebuke, and exhort"(2 Timothy 4:2). And this divine arrangement is to continue. Romans 10:13-15:

For "everyone who calls on the name of the Lord will be saved." How then will they call on him in whom they have not believed? And how are they to believe in him of whom they have never heard? And how are they to hear without someone preaching? And how are they to preach unless they are sent? As it is written, "How beautiful are the feet of those who preach the good news!"

1 Corinthians 1:21: "It pleased God through the folly of what we preach to save those who believe." Romans 10:17: "So faith comes from hearing, and hearing through the word of Christ." Therefore, according to Rom. 10:6-8:

Let no one say, "Who will ascend into heaven (that is to bring Christ down)," or "Who will descend into the abyss?'" (that is, to bring Christ up from the dead). But what does it say? "The word is near you, in your mouth and in your heart" (that is, the word of faith that we proclaim).

This then is evidently God's order of the application of divine Grace.

And yet, notwithstanding these plain declarations, men try all sorts of measures and methods to bring Christ near, because they cannot understand that when they have the Word, they have the Spirit, and when they have the Spirit, they have Christ. In Luke 11:27, we read how a woman called down a blessing on the mother of our Lord because she was privileged to have borne Him. But Jesus answered, "Blessed rather are they who hear the word of God and keep it." That Word carries the Spirit to the hearer, and through it converts the sinner and sanctifies the saint. In the Acts of the Apostles also we read how again and again the Spirit was given through and in connection with the Word. The Apostles depended on nothing but Word and Sacrament. The Lutheran doctrine, then, that the Word of God is the great effectual means of Grace; that it is the vehicle and instrument of the Holy Spirit; that through it, the Spirit renews the soul, applies forgiveness, and sanctifies the hearer or reader more and more—is the pure truth of Christ.

Hence, wherever the Lutheran Church is true to her name and faith, she preaches the whole counsel of God, and relies on that for ingathering and upbuilding. A true Lutheran pulpit cannot be a sensational pulpit, for discoursing wordly wisdom, philosophy, poetry, or politics. It must expound the Word, and never gets done preaching repentance towards God and faith in our Lord Jesus Christ. What a beautiful and harmonious system of God's methods of saving men is thus brought into view! How helpful to the sinner desiring salvation! Instead of waiting and hoping and dreaming of something wonderful to happen to bring him into the kingdom, he needs only to go to the divine Word and let that Word do its work in his heart.

Though all the world with devils filled
Should threaten to undo us
We will not fear for God hath willed
His truth to triumph through us
Thy Word above all earthly powers
No thanks to them, abideth
The Spirit and the gifts are ours
Through him who with us sideth
Let goods and kindred go
This mortal life also
The body they may kill
God's truth abideth still
His kingdom is forever

18

Conversion: Its Nature and Necessity

CLOSELY related to the doctrine of the power, or efficacy, of the divine Word—as considered in the last chapter—is the doctrine of conversion. It is the subject of conversion, therefore, that we are now going to examine. It is an important subject. It deserves a prominent place in treating of the Way of Salvation. It is also an intensely personal subject. Each one who desires to be in the Way of Salvation is personally interested in it. The eternal destiny of every one who reads these pages is closely connected with the question whether or not he is converted. To be in an unconverted state, is to be in a state of great peril. The issues of eternity are involved in the final decision of the soul, in reference to this great subject. It is of the most vital importance, therefore, that each one examine and understand it.

And yet, strange as it may seem, there are few subjects concerning which those interested are more in the dark. Stranger still, often those who preach and talk most about it, who are loudest in proclaiming its necessity, know least about it. Ask its existence; and they give at best very confused and unscriptural answers. We therefore propose to examine it in the light of the Word of God, and may He, the Spirit of truth, enable us to know and believe its divine teachings!

What then is conversion? The original and simple meaning of the word convert is to turn —to turn around. This is also the meaning of the Latin word from which the English comes. The Greek word, which in the New Testament is translated "convert" or "conversion," also refers to the act of turning. It is translated in this way quite frequently. Thus the same Greek word that is in some places translated convert, is in other places translated turned, as in Mark 5:30: "Jesus...turned him about in the press." Acts 16:18: "But Paul...turned and said." Matthew 12:44: "I will return into my house." Acts 26:18: "To turn them from darkness to light." And so in many other places. It is plain, then, that the meaning of the word is a turning or facing about— a returning, or a changing of direction—as if a traveler, on finding himself going the wrong way, turns, returns, changes his course, comes back, he converts himself.[5]

Applying this word now to a moral or religious use, it means a turning from sin to righteousness, from Satan to God. The transgressor who had been walking in the way of disobedience and enmity against God and towards eternal death, is turned about into the way of righteousness, towards eternal life. This is a change of direction, but it is also something more. It is a change of state—from a state of sin to a state of Grace. It is still more. It is a change of nature—from a sinner unto a saint. It is finally a change of relation—from an outcast and stranger unto a child and heir. Thus there is an outward and an inward turning, a complete change. That this is the scriptural meaning of conversion is very clear from Acts 26:18. The Lord is about to send Paul to the Gentiles for the purpose of converting them. He describes the work of conversion thus:

That they may turn from darkness to light and from the power of Satan to God, that they may receive forgiveness of sins and a place among those who are sanctified by faith in me.

As already remarked, the word here translated to "turn" is the same that is elsewhere translated to "convert." If we now inquire more particularly into the nature or process of this change which is called "conversion," we find in it two constituent elements. The one is penitence or contrition, the

---

[5] For an examination and application of Bible examples of Conversion, see the book "New Testament Conversions."

other is faith. Taken together, they make up conversion. In passing, we may briefly notice that sometimes the Scriptures use the word "repentance" as embracing both penitence and faith, thus making it synonymous with conversion. Penitence or contrition, as the first part of conversion, is sorrow for sin. It is a realizing sense of the nature and guilt of sin, of its heinousness and its damnable character. True penitence is indeed a painful experience. A penitent heart is, therefore, called "a broken and a contrite heart." It takes from the sinner his self-satisfaction and false peace. It makes him restless, dissatisfied and troubled. Instead of loving and delighting in sin, it makes him hate sin and turn from it with aversion. It brings the sinner low in the dust. He cries out, "I am vile;" "I loathe myself;" "God be merciful to me a sinner." This is the penitence insisted on by the prophets, breathed forth in the penitential psalms, preached by John the Baptist, by Christ and by all His apostles. It is not necessary to quote passages in proof of this. Every Bible reader knows that the Word is full of exhortations to such sorrow and repenting for sin.

But penitence must not stop with hating and bemoaning sin, and longing for deliverance. The penitent sinner must resolutely turn from sin towards Jesus Christ the Savior. He must believe that He took upon Himself the punishment due to his sins, and by His death atoned for them; that He satisfied a violated law, and an offended Law-giver; that thus He has become his Substitute and Redeemer, and has taken away all his sins. This the penitent must believe. Thus must he cast himself upon Christ, and trust in Him with a childlike confidence, knowing that he is justified by faith, and he has "peace with God" (Romans 5:1). True penitence always grows into faith, and true faith always presupposes penitence. Where one is, there the other is: and where both are, there is conversion. Penitence, therefore, is not something that goes before conversion, and faith something that follows after, and conversion an indefinable something sandwiched in between, as some seem to imagine; but penitence and faith are the constituent elements that make up conversion.

In the next place we would inquire: Who needs this change? We answer, first, all who are not in a state of loving obedience to God; that is, all who are not turned away from and against sin and Satan, and turned toward holiness and God. On the other hand, all who really hate sin, mourn over it, strive against it, trust in and cling to Christ as their personal Redeemer, need no conversion. No matter whether they can tell where and when and how they were converted or not. All who know by blessed experience that they now have in their hearts the elements of penitence and faith, are in a state of conversion, and if they earnestly ask God they may have the assurance that their sins are forgiven and that they are accepted in the Beloved. True, this assurance may sometimes be dimmed by doubt or under the strain of strong temptation; but as long as there is real hatred of sin and an earnest desire to rest in Christ alone, there is Grace and acceptance with Christ.

To the class of those who are in a converted state belong those baptized children of the Church who have kept their baptismal covenant. Given to Christ in holy baptism, the seeds of the new life implanted through that divine ordinance, reared and trained by Christian parents or guardians, they have belonged to Christ from their childhood. From their earliest years they have hated sin, repented of it, trusted in Christ, and loved Him. They are "turned from darkness to light and from the power of Satan to God." They need only that daily dying to sin, and that daily turning to Christ, which all Christians need on account of the sins and infirmities of the flesh which still cleave to them. Such were Joseph, and Samuel, and the covenant, and therefore children of God. Of this class we have written in former chapters. We need not enlarge on them here. They need no conversion, because they are in a converted state. Yet there are well-meaning people, who have more zeal than knowledge, who would violently exhort even such to be converted. Thus would they confuse them, distract them, unsettle their faith in Christ, quench the Spirit, and, perhaps, drive them to unbelief and despair. From all such teachers, we pray: "Good Lord, deliver us."

19

Varies Phenomena of Experiences

WE have spoken of the meaning of this term, inquired into the nature of the change, and noted its essential elements. We have also learned that there are some who do not need it because they are in a converted state, and that all who are not in such a state of Grace, do need conversion, regardless of anything that may or may not have taken place in the past. We now look into to the agencies or means by which this change happens. For it is a change which man can certainly not effect by his own efforts. Of this change it can certainly be said that it is "not by might, not by power, but by my Spirit, says the Lord"(Zechariah 4:6). To have this change brought about in the heart, all need to pray in the words of the Psalmist, Psalm 85:4, "Restore us again, O God of our salvation, and put away your indignation toward us." It is God the Holy Ghost who must work this change in the soul. This He does through His own life-giving Word. It is the office of that Word, as the organ of the Holy Spirit, to bring about a knowledge of sin, to awaken sorrow and contrition, and to make the sinner hate and turn from his sin. That same Word then directs the sinner to Him who came to save him from sin. It takes him to the cross, it enables him to believe that his sins were all atoned for there, and that, therefore, he is not condemned. In other words, the Word of God awakens and constantly deepens true penitence.

It also begets and constantly increases true faith. Or, in one word, it converts the sinner. Of this wonderful power and efficacy in the Word, we have already fully written, so that we need not enter upon this again. To the Word, then, let the unconverted sinner go. Let him be careful to put no barrier in the way of its influence. Let him permit it to have free course, and it will do its own blessed work. We desire now to notice and to call special attention to the diversified phenomena and experiences incident to this change. There are some, indeed, who will not admit that there are any variations. They would measure all by the same standard, and that standard often a very abnormal one. With some, the only standard is their own distorted experience. In their pharisaic self-righteousness they are ready to assert that every one whose experience does not in every respect conform to their own is not converted. The writer has frequently, in his pastoral work, met poor, downcast souls, who were groping in the dark, bemoaning themselves, and living a cheerless life, because they had been taught that, as they had not had an experience just like somebody else, they were not converted, and had neither part nor lot in the kingdom of God. He has also met more than one who, by just such vagaries and delusions, had been driven to unbelief and despair. And what a relief it often is to such poor, benighted ones, if they are not too far gone, to be led out of their vain imaginings into the blessed light of God's truth.

We notice, first, that not all conversions are alike clearly marked. Some are more strongly marked than others. Some are more intense than others. The degree of intensity or depth of experience, may depend on several things. It may depend, to a certain extent, on the temperament of the individual. One person is of a phlegmatic temperament; his mind is sluggish; his feelings are not deep; he rarely becomes excited. Of a cool, calculating disposition, he does everything deliberately and cautiously. He feels the ground before him every time he takes a step. When God's Word comes to such a person it does not generally revolutionize him at once. He hears it, carries it home, weighs it, ponders it, and wants to hear more. Gradually, slowly, his mind is enlightened, his heart is moved, his will is changed. In him the Word is likely to grow as a seed, or operate like leaven in meal. There is seldom much excitement, and little outward manifestation.

Another is of a sanguine temperament; he is impulsive, easily aroused, and ready to jump at conclusions. When God's Word comes to him, and is not willfully opposed, it is likely to take a strong hold of him. It may so alarm him and take away his peace that he may at once see the depth of his guilt. Again, when Christ, His atonement and love for guilty men are presented he may quickly lay hold of the hope set before him in the Gospel, and rest himself entirely on Christ. God's Word comes to him like a hammer that breaks the stony heart. Both people have been led by the same Spirit, through the same Word. Both have repented and believed, but each in his own way.

The degree of intensity may also depend on the former life of the person. One has wandered very far from his Father's house. He has wasted his substance in rebellious living. He has sunken very low in sin and guilt. When God's Word comes to such a person, and shows him his wretched state, when he comes to himself, his penitence is likely to be deep and painful, and when he is enabled to believe, his faith will probably be quite joyful, because he realizes the depth from which he was drawn. God's Word has acted on him like a fire, burning deep down into the conscience, consuming its waste. Another has never wandered so far away. He has all along been brought up in the true faith. He was baptized as a child and has learned Christian values. He has observed the outward obligations of religion, though he may not in the past have given himself unreservedly unto Christ. When such a person does give himself to God, his repentance may not be so clear, or his faith be so demonstrative, but on this account the conversion is none the less real. God's Word, at length, opened his heart, as the heart of Lydia, the seller of purple, was opened.

We notice in the next place that there are differences in the length of the process. With some the process lasts longer than with others. This fact is implied indeed in the variations noted above. On one person the Word may make but a superficial impression at first. It may be only a slight dissatisfaction with self. But with more light and knowledge, the feeling of penitence is deepened. Longings for something better are awakened. Yearnings and outcryings after deliverance arise from the heart. There is then at first only a timid trembling look to Christ. Gradually, slowly, the faith is drawn out, until the heart is enabled to cast itself on the Savior and rest trustingly there. It may be weeks, months, or even years, before that penitent one comes out into the clear sunlight of assurance and peace. In all such cases it is "first the blade, then the ear, and then the full corn in the ear."

On the other hand, we freely admit that there are sudden conversions. God's word comes as a hammer or as a fire (Jeremiah 23:29). It smites and burns until the sinner is brought low in the dust. The heart is broken and becomes contrite and ready to lay hold of the Crucified One, as soon as He is presented. To this class generally, belong some of those noted above who are of a sanguine temperament, and those who have fallen deeply into sin. Going to the Word of God for examples of the two latter classes, we might mention Zaccheus, Saul of Tarsus, the Philippian jailer, and the three thousand on the day of Pentecost, as cases of sudden conversion—while we might instance the disciples of Christ in general, as cases of slow and gradual conversion. 1 Corinthians 12:6: "there are varieties of activities, but it is the same God who empowers them all in everyone." Zaccheus and the Jailor, and Saul, and the three thousand, would doubtless always remember and be able to tell about the time and place and circumstances of their entrance into the kingdom.

But could the apostles of Jesus tell? Do we not read how slowly they were enlightened; how, little by little, their errors had to be removed, and the truth applied? They did not, in fact, become established in the faith until after the resurrection. And so it is with many, probably indeed, with most of the very best Christians in the church today. They cannot tell when they were converted. Neither is it necessary. On the Day of Judgment the question will not be asked: "Where and when and how were you converted!" The question will be, "Were you in a converted state, turned from darkness to light, and from the power of Satan to God?" No matter whether you belonged to that favored class who kept their baptismal covenant unbroken; or whether, after you had been a stranger and a foreigner for a time, you were slowly and through much doubt and misgiving brought to penitence and faith; or whether you were suddenly brought into the kingdom. Can each one then tell whether he is at present in a converted state or not? We answer unhesitatingly, Yes, to a certainty. The inquirer need only look into his heart and see how his sins affect him. Do his sins grieve him? Does he hate them?

Does he earnestly long and strive to be rid of them? Does he daily turn to Jesus Christ for forgiveness and strength? If he can answer these questions in the affirmative, he has the elements and evidences of conversion and the new life.

Though faith be weak, it is accepted. Though assurance at times be dim, the vision of faith clouded, and faith itself almost unconscious, it still saves; for it is not the assurance, but the faith, that justifies. But if, on the other hand, his sins do not trouble the sinner; if they are as trifles to him; if they do not daily drive him to the Cross, the elements and evidences of the new life are certainly wanting. Such a person is in an unconverted state. And let not such a person delude himself with the false idea that something, which he called change, had taken place at some point in the past. He can know whether he is *now* in the faith. It is poor theology, it is altogether anti scriptural, for a Christian to go through the world singing plaintively:

Tis a point I long to know;
Oft it causes anxious thought,
Do I love the Lord, or no?
Am I His, or am I not?

He whose faith, reaching up out of a heart that mourns over and hates sin, lays hold of Christ, even tremblingly, can say, "I know in whom I have believed," "I know that my Redeemer lives." He can joyfully sing:

I know that my Redeemer lives!
What comfort this sweet sentence gives!
He lives, He lives, who once was dead,
He lives, my ever-living Head.
He lives to bless me with His love,
He lives to plead for me above,
He lives my hungry soul to feed,
He lives to help in time of need.
He lives to silence all my fears,
He lives to wipe away my tears,
He lives to calm my troubled heart,
He lives all blessings to impart.

He lives, all glory to His Name!
He lives, my Jesus, still the same;
Oh the sweet joy this sentence gives,
I know that my Redeemer lives!

20

Human Agency in Conversion

WHAT is part and responsibility of the human will in this matter? Before we leave the subject of conversion, it is important that we consider and understand this question. For on this point also grievous and dangerous views and practices prevail. Human nature tends to go to extremes. Here, too, there is a tendency to go too far, either in the one direction or in the other. There are those, on the one hand, who virtually and practically make this change of heart and of nature a human work. They practically leave out the agency of the Holy Spirit, or His means of Grace. On the other hand, there are those whose ideas and teachings would rid man of all responsibility in the matter, and make of him a mere machine, that is irresistibly moved and controlled from above. Is either of these views correct and scriptural? If not, what is the Bible doctrine on this subject? What has the human will— i.e., the choosing and determining faculty of the mind, to do with conversion? If it is a factor, to what extent? Where does its activity begin or end? In how far is the human will responsible for the accomplishment or non-accomplishment of this change?

These questions we shall endeavor briefly and plainly to answer. We must necessarily return to man as he is before his conversion, while still in his natural, sinful, unrenewed state. In this state of sin, the will shares, in common with all the other parts of his being, in the ruin and corruption resulting from the fall. The natural man has the "understanding darkened;"(Ephesians 4:18) "is alienated from the life of God, through the ignorance that is in him, because of the blindness of his heart"(Ephesians 4:18). He "does not accept the things of the Spirit of God, for they are folly to him, and he is not able to understand them because they are spiritually discerned"(1 Corinthians 2:14). He is "in darkness," "dead in trespasses and sins"(Ephesians 2:1). Thus is the whole man in darkness, blindness, ignorance, bondage to Satan, and at enmity with God. He is in a state of spiritual death. The will is equally affected by this total depravity. If the natural man cannot even see, discern, or know the things of the Spirit, how much less can he will to do them! Before his conversion, man is utterly impotent "to will or to do" anything towards his renewal.

The strong words of Luther, as quoted in the Formula of Concord, are strictly scriptural:

In spiritual and divine things which pertain to the salvation of the soul, man is like a pillar of salt, like Lot's wife, yea, like a log and a stone, like a lifeless statue, which uses neither eyes nor mouth, neither senses nor heart (Matthew 3:9).

But that same God who could, out of the very stones, raise up spiritual children to Abraham, can also change the stony heart of man, and put life into those who were dead in trespasses and sins. The first movement, however, must always be from God to the sinner, and not from the sinner to God. God does, indeed, in His great mercy, come first to us. This He does through His own means of Grace. In holy baptism He meets us even on the threshold of existence, takes us into His loving arms, places His hands in blessing upon our heads, breathes life into us, and adopts us into His own family. If the sinner later falls away from Baptismal grace, and goes back into the ways of sin, and breaks his side of the covenant, God is still faithful and comes to him again by His Holy Spirit through His Word; strives with him and endeavors to turn or convert him again from darkness to light, and from the power of Satan unto God.

We should notice here a distinction between those, who have at some time been under divine influence, as by virtue of the sacramental Word in baptism, or through the written or preached Word, and those who have never been touched by a breath from above. When the Spirit of God comes to the former, He finds something still to appeal to. There is more or less receptivity to receive the Grace of God, as there is more or less life still in the germ formerly implanted. When He comes to the latter class there is nothing to work on. The foundations must be laid. A receptivity must be brought about, a new life must be inbreathed. In other words, in the conversion of the latter the Holy Spirit must do what He has already done in the former. The one is the conversion of a once regenerate but now lapsed one. The other is the regeneration and conversion of one heretofore always dead in sin. But in every case, God comes first to the sinner; whether it be in the sacramental, or the written, or the preached, or the pondered Word. It is always through that Word, as we have already shown, that the spirit of God operates on the sinful heart, enkindling penitence and begetting faith in Christ.

Now, what part does the will perform in this great work? Is it entirely passive, merely wrought upon, as the stone by the sculptor? At first, the will is doubtless entirely passive. The first movements, the first desires, the first serious thoughts, are beyond question produced by the Spirit, through the Word. These are the advance signals and heralds of Grace. They are the preparatory steps, and hence these first approaches of divine influence are called by theologians Prevenient Grace, that is the divine influence of Grace which precedes or goes before all other movements in the return of the soul to God. This preparatory Grace sometimes comes to the sinner unsought, whatever to do with the first beginnings of conversion. Of this our Confessions testify: "God must first come to us." "Man's will hath no power to work the righteousness of God, or a spiritual righteousness, without the spirit of God." Of this the Prophet speaks when he says, Zechariah 4:6, "Not by might, nor by power, but by my Spirit, says the Lord." Also, 1 Corinthians 12:3, "No one can say that 'Jesus is the Lord,' except in the Holy Spirit."

After prevenient Grace, however, begins to make itself felt, then the will begins to take part.[6] It must now assume an attitude, and meet the question: Shall I yield to these holy influences or not? One or the other of two courses must be pursued. There must be a yielding to the heavenly strivings, or a resistance. To resist at this point requires a positive act of the will. This act man can put forth by his own strength. On the other hand, with the help of that Grace, already at work in his heart, he can refuse to put forth that act of his will, and thus remain non-resistant. If man, thus influenced from above, now deliberately uses his will power, and resists the gracious influences of prevenient Grace, he quenches the Holy Spirit of God, whereby he is sealed to the day of redemption. He has hardened his heart. His last state is worse than the first. He remains unconverted, and on himself alone is the responsibility. If, on the other hand, he even with the assistance of prevenient Grace, permits it to do its work, the process goes on. His will is being renewed. It experiences the pulsations of a new life. It realizes the possession of new powers. There is an infusion from God's will into his will, and now prevenient Grace is changed into operating Grace. The Word has free course. It runs and is glorified. He "works out his own salvation with fear and trembling,"(Philippians 2:12) while all the time "God that works in him both to will and to work according to his good pleasure." Such a person is a new creature in Christ Jesus. Operative Grace goes out into co-operating Grace. He becomes a worker with God, and as he grows in Grace and knowledge, his will becomes more free as it comes into harmony with God's will. Again, we ask, what does the human will have to do with this change?

We answer: Two things. First, man can will to go to church where the means of Grace are, or he can will to remain away. If he deliberately wills to keep himself away from where their influence is exerted, he remains unconverted, and the blame for his non-conversion is on himself. If, on the other hand, he wills to go where God speaks to man in His ordinary way, he

---

[6] *Editor's note. Gerberding disagrees with the Waltherian perspective on this issue which characterized many American Lutheran churches such as the Missouri and Wisconsin Synods. Walther argues that the will does not in any sense cooperate in conversion, as explained in Luther's well-known work *The Bondage of the Will*. I disagree with Gerberding on this point.

does so much towards permitting God to convert him. Secondly, when the means of Grace do carry renewing power, and he is made to realize their efficacy—though it is at first only in an uneasiness, dissatisfaction with self, and an undefined longing after something better—he can, as we have seen, permit the work to go on. Thus he may be said, negatively, to help towards his conversion. On the other hand, he can shake off the good impressions, tear away from the holy influences, resist the Spirit, and remain unconverted. Clearly, on him is all the responsibility if he perishes. God desired to convert him. He "rejected the purpose of God against himself." Luke 7:30.

And thus our Lutheran doctrine of Grace through the means of Grace, clears away all difficulties and avoids all contradictions. It gives God all the glory and throws on man all the responsibility. Sailing thus under the colors of scriptural doctrine, we steer clear of the Scylla of Calvinism on the one hand, and also escape the Charybdis of Arminianism on the other. We give to Sovereign Grace all the glory of our salvation just as much as the Calvinists do. And yet we make salvation as free as the boldest Arminian does. Whatever is excellent in both systems we retain. Whatever is false in both we reject. We refuse to make of man a machine, who is irresistibly brought into the kingdom of God, and forced indeed to accept of Sovereign Grace. On the other hand, we utterly repudiate the idea that man is himself able to "get religion," to "get through," to "grasp the blessing," or to "save himself." To such self-exaltation we give no place—no, not for a moment! But that,

The Holy Spirit hath called me by His Gospel, enlightened me by His gifts, and sanctified and preserved me in the true faith; in like manner as He calls, gathers, enlightens, and sanctifies the whole Christian Church on earth, and preserves it in union with Jesus Christ in the true faith. In which Christian Church He daily forgives me abundantly all my sins and the sins of all believers, and will raise up me and all the dead at the last day, and will grant everlasting life to me and to all who believe in Christ. This is most certainly true.

Grace first contrived the way
To save rebellious man;
And all the steps that Grace display

Which drew the wondrous plan.
Grace taught my roving feet
To tread the heavenly road;
And new supplies each hour I meet,
While pressing on to God.
Grace all the work shall crown
Through everlasting days;
It lays in heaven the topmost stone,
And well deserves the praise.

21

Justification

AMONG all the doctrines of our holy Christian faith, the doctrine of Justification by faith alone, stands most prominent. Luther calls it: "The doctrine upon which the church stands or falls," i.e., as a church holds fast and appropriates this doctrine she remains pure and firm, and as she departs from it, she becomes corrupt and falls. This doctrine was the turning point of the Reformation in the sixteenth century. It was the experience of its necessity and efficacy that made Luther what he was, and equipped him for a Reformer. Naturally, therefore, it occupies the chief place in all our Confessions, and is prominent in all the history of our Church. In these chapters on the "Way of Salvation," it has been implied throughout. There is indeed no doctrine of salvation that is not more or less connected with or dependent on this one. Some time ago we noticed the statement of a certain bishop in a large Protestant Church, declaring that: "not Justification, but the Divinity of Christ, is the great fundamental doctrine that conditions the standing or falling church." At first glance, this may seem plausible. But when we reflect on it, we begin to see that the true doctrine concerning the Person of Christ is not only implied, but embraced in the doctrine of Justification by Faith.

A man might be sound on the Divinity of Christ, and yet not know aright the Way of Salvation. But a man cannot be sound on Justification without being sound, not only on the Person of Christ, but also on His work and the Way of Salvation through Him. So much has been written and preached in our Church on this subject, that it is not necessary for us to enter upon a full discussion here. We will endeavor, therefore, merely in outline, to call attention to a few of its most prominent and practical features. We inquire briefly into its meaning and nature. Justification is an act of God, by which He accounts or judges a person to be righteous in His sight. It is not a change in the person's nature, but it is a change in his standing in the sight of God. Before justification he stands in the sight of God, guilty and condemned. Through justification, he stands before God free from guilt and condemnation; he is acquitted, released, regarded and treated as if he had never been guilty or condemned. The justified person stands in the sight of God, as if he really had never committed a sin and were perfectly innocent. Thus it is clear that justification treats of and has regard to the sinner's relation to God. It has nothing to do with his change of nature. It is of the utmost importance that this be kept constantly in mind. It is by applying justification to the change in the sinner's nature that so many become confused, and fall into grievous and dangerous errors.

The original source, or moving cause of justification, is God's love. Had God not "loved the world" there would have been no divine planning or counseling for man's justification. Truly it required a divine mind to originate a scheme by which God "could be just and yet justify the ungodly." All the wisdom of the world could never have answered the question: "How can mortal man be just with God?" Man stood, in the sight of God as a rebel against His divine authority, a transgressor of divine law, guilty, condemned and wholly unable to justify himself, or to answer for one in a thousand offences. God had given His word that, because of guilt, there must be punishment and suffering. This word was given before sin was committed, and was repeated a thousand times afterwards. There must then be obedience to an infinite law, or infinite punishment for transgression. How could this gulf be bridged, and man saved? There was only one way. "God so loved the world that He gave His only-begotten Son"(John 3:16). That Son, "the brightness of the Father's glory and the express image of His person," "in him the whole fullness of deity dwells bodily,"(Colossians 2:8) came into our world. He came to take the sinner's place—to be his substitute. Though Lord and giver of the law, He put Himself under the law. He fulfilled it in every jot and tittle. He did no sin, neither was guile found in his mouth. Thus He worked out a complete and perfect righteousness. He did not need this righteousness for Himself, for He had a righteousness far above the righteousness of the letter of law. He wrought it out not for Himself, but for man, that He might make it over and impute it to the transgressor. Thus then while man had no obedience of his own, he could have the obedience of another set down to his account, as though it were his own.

But this was not enough. Man had sinned and was still constantly sinning, his very nature being a sinful one. As already noted, the divine Word was pledged that there must be punishment for sin. The Son, who came to be a substitute, said: Put me in the sinner's place; let me be the guilty one; let the blows fall upon me. And thus, He "who knew no sin was made sin (or a sin-offering) for us." (2 Corinthians 5:21) He "was made a curse,"(Galatians 3:13) "bore our sins,"(1 Peter 2:24) and "the iniquity of us all"(Isaiah 53:6). He, the God-man, was regarded as the guilty one, treated as the guilty one, suffered as the guilty one. He suffered as God, as well as man. For the Divine and human were inseparably united in one person. Divinity by itself cannot suffer and die. But thus mysteriously connected with the humanity it could and really did participate in the suffering and dying. God suffered through His human nature. And so God really suffered. Who could possibly calculate what Immanuel could have suffered? What must that suffering have been when it crushed Him to earth, made Him cry out so plaintively, and at last took His life! Our old theologians loved to say, that what the sufferings of Christ lacked in extensiveness or duration, they made up in intensiveness.

Thus there was a perfect atonement. All the punishment had been endured. A perfect righteousness had been wrought out, and the Father set His seal to it in the resurrection and ascension of His dear Son. Here, then, was real substitution, and this is the ground for our justification. It has been asked, on this point, if Christ by His perfect life wrought out a complete righteousness, which He needed not for Himself, but intended for the sinner, why wasn't this sufficient? Why was His death necessary? On the other hand, if His death is a perfect atonement for all sin, why does the sinner, in addition to a full and free forgiveness, procured by the death of Christ, need also the application of the righteousness of the life of Christ? In a word, why are both the life and death necessary to justify the sinner? We answer: By His death or suffering obedience, He worked out a negative righteousness, the forgiveness of sins. By His life, or active obedience, He won a positive righteousness. The former releases from punishment. The latter confers character, standing and honor in the kingdom of God.

To illustrate: Two persons have broken the laws of their land, are guilty, condemned, and suffer the penalty in prison. To one comes a message of pardon from the king. The prison doors are opened and he goes forth a free man. The law cannot again seize him and condemn him for the crimes of which he is pardoned. But as he goes forth among his fellow men he realizes that though released from punishment, and negatively righteous, he has no standing, no character, no positive righteousness, unless he earn and merit it for his king. In addition to pardon, or release from punishment, he is assured that his king has adopted him as his son, will take him into his family and endow him with his name and all the privileges of his house. Now this pardoned one has a double righteousness. Negatively, pardon and release from punishment; positively, a name, standing, character, honor, and the richest endowments of the kingdom. Even thus has the Son of God wrought out for us a two-fold righteousness, viz.: Negatively, by His sufferings and death He purchased for the believer the forgiveness of sin and release from punishment; and positively, by His life of obedience He secured and imparts to the sinner a perfect righteousness, a name and a place in His kingdom, with all its honors and blessings.

In the procuring of this double righteousness, Christ worked out first the positive and then the negative. In the conferring of it He gives first the negative and then the positive. And therefore the two-fold message of consolation. Isaiah 40:1-2:

Comfort, comfort my people, says your God. Speak tenderly to Jerusalem, and cry to her that her warfare is ended, that her iniquity is pardoned, that she has received from the LORD's hand double for all her sins.

This justification has been purchased and paid for. But it is not yet applied. The sinner has not yet appropriated it and made it his own. How is this to be done? We answer: By Faith. Faith is the eye that looks to Christ. It sees His perfect atonement and His spotless righteousness. It is, at the same time, the hand that reaches out, lays hold of Christ, and clings to Him as the only help and the only hope. This faith, springing from a penitent heart, that realizes its own unworthiness and guiltiness, renouncing all claim to merit or self-righteousness, casts itself on the divine Savior, trusts implicitly in Him, and rests there.

This faith justifies. Not because it is an act that merits or earns justification. No! In no sense. Christ has earned it. Faith only lays hold of and appropriates Christ and a "gift of God," as the Scriptures declare. He that has the faith is justified, acquitted, forgiven. The appropriation or application, is when we believe with all the heart on the Son of God. This faith is not a mere historical or intellectual belief. It is a living thing. Yet it is not its livingness that justifies. The justifying element is that it grasps and holds Christ. Christ really justifies. Faith justifies in so far as it grasps, holds, rests in and trusts in Christ alone. Such, in brief, is the Lutheran doctrine of "Justification by Faith." We have not thought it necessary to quote from the Augsburg Confession or the Formula of Concord for proof. Neither is it necessary or desirable that we lengthen out this chapter with quotations from standard theologians. Any one desiring further proof or amplification can find abundance of it in all our Confessions, and in all recognized writers in the Church. Nor have we taken up the space with Scripture quotations.

To quote all that the Bible says on the subject would be to transcribe a large proportion of its passages. It would necessitate especially writing out of a large part of the writings of Paul, who makes it the great theme of several of his epistles. Every devout reader of Paul's letters will find this great doctrine shining forth in almost every chapter, so much so that the Roman Bishop who was driven by Luther to a study of the New Testament threw down his book and said: "Paul also has become a Lutheran!" In conclusion, we desire to impress one thought. The doctrine of Justification is so highly prized by the believer, not so much because of the grand and matchless scheme it brings to light, as because of the peace and comfort it has brought into his heart. The one who truly embraces this doctrine, realizes its efficacy and power. It is precious to him, above all things, as a matter of personal experience. This experience is not the doctrine, but the result of receiving the doctrine. He has realized the blessedness of having his own sins forgiven, his transgressions covered. Being justified by faith, he has peace with God through our Lord Jesus Christ. This blessed experience was the root and spring of Luther's courage and strength. Luther's inner experience fitted him to become the Reformer. Without it all his other gifts and qualifications would not have availed.

Let Sunday School teachers, church-workers and ministers examine themselves. Without this heart-experience, all theorizing about the doctrine is vain. Such a scriptural experience never develops a Pharisee. It never runs into self-exaltations. It constantly exalts and magnifies Christ. It habitually humbles self. It lays the self low at the foot of the cross, and it remains there. Not that it is a gloomy or despondent spirit. For while it constantly mourns over the imperfections and sins of self, it, at the same time, constantly rejoices in the full and perfect salvation of Christ. While it never ceases in this life to shed the tears of penitence, it also never ceases to sing the joyful song of deliverance. It develops a Christian after the type of a Paul, a Luther, a Gerhard and a Francke. Blessed is he who understands and experiences justification by faith. Doubly sad the state of him who has the doctrine, without its experience and peace and glory.

Jesus, Thy Blood and Righteousness
Thy beauty are, my glorious dress;
Midst flaming worlds, in these arrayed,
With joy shall I lift up my head.
Bold shall I stand in that great day,
For who aught to my charge shall lay?
Fully through these absolved I am
From sin and fear, from guilt and shame.
This spotless robe the same appears,
When ruined nature sinks in years:

JUSTIFICATION

No age can change its constant hue;
Thy Blood preserves it ever new.
Oh let the dead now hear
Thy voice; Now bid
Thy banished ones rejoice!
Their beauty this, their glorious dress,
Righteousness.

22

Sanctification

IN the last chapter we showed that the doctrine of justification deals with the sinner's change of relation, or change of state. We also learned that faith is the instrumental or applying cause of justification. In another place we showed that true faith presupposes penitence, and this again presupposes a sense and knowledge of sin. Again we showed that repentance and faith are the two essential elements of conversion; that where these elements are found there is a change of heart, and the beginning of a new life. This new life is, however, only in its germ. These new actions. A new light has come into the intellect; a new love into the heart and a new bent into the will, and so a new creature with a new life.

This newness is of a germinal or seed character. Now it belongs to the very nature of life to develop, to increase, and to make progress. And it is this development or growth of the new life that we wish now to consider. It is called sanctification, or the growth of the soul the righteousness of Christ. In sanctification, God imparts the image of a holy God. It is closely related to justification, and yet clearly distinct from it. In justification, God imputes or counts over to the sinner the righteousness of the new life. Justification is what God does *for* the believer; sanctification is what His Spirit does *in* him. Justification being purely an act of God, is instantaneous and complete; sanctification being a work in which man has a share, is progressive. Justification takes away the guilt of sin; sanctification gradually takes away its power. Sanctification begins with justification.

So soon as the sinner believes he is justified; but just so soon as he believes, he also has the beginnings of a new life. In time, therefore, the two come together; but in thought they are distinct. And it is of the greatest importance that these distinctions be understood and kept in mind. It is by confounding justification with sanctification, and vice versa, that all the flagrant, soul-endangering errors concerning the so-called "higher life," "sinless perfection," and "holiness," are promulgated and believed. It is by quoting Scripture passages that speak of justification and applying them to sanctification, that this delusion is strengthened. How often have we not heard that precious passage, 1 John 1:7 "The blood of Jesus his Son cleanses us from all sin," quoted to prove entire sanctification. Now, if we understand the Scriptures at all, that passage speaks of the forgiveness of sin through the efficacy of Christ's blood, and not of overcoming sin in the believer, or eradicating its very fibers and impulses.

Let us understand clearly what we mean by sanctification. The English word comes from a Latin word that means sacred, consecrated, devoted to holy purposes. The Greek word translated "sanctify" in our English Bible also means to separate from common and set apart for holy purposes. The same word that is translated sanctify, is in many places translated consecrate, or make holy. The English word saint comes from the same Latin root, and is translated from the same Greek root, as sanctify. A saint means a sanctified one, or one who is being sanctified. Thus we find believers called saints or sanctified ones. We find, indeed, that the apostles call all the members of their churches saints. Thus they speak of "the churches of the saints"(1 Corinthians 14:33). So also in many other passages.

In harmony with the apostolic usage, we confess in the Apostles' Creed: "I believe in the Holy Christian Church (which is) the communion—or community—of saints." If then saints means sanctified ones, or holy persons, do the Bible and the Apostles' Creed demand perfect sinlessness? By no means! Christians are indeed to strive to constantly become more and more free from sin. They are "called to be saints,"(1 Corinthians 1:2) are constantly being sanctified or made holy. But their sanctity or holiness is only relative.

They have indeed "come out from the world," to "be separate"(2 Corinthians 6:17). They are "a peculiar people"(1 Peter 2:9). They hate sin, repent of it, flee from it, strive against it, and overcome it more and more. They "mortify the deeds of the body,"(Romans 8:13) "keep it under,"(1 Corinthians 9:27) "crucify the flesh with its affections and lusts,"(Galatians 5:24) "present—(or consecrate)—their bodies, as living sacrifices to God"(Romans 12:1). They have pledged themselves at Christ's altar to "renounce the devil and all his works and ways, the vanities of the world and the sinful desires of the flesh, and to live up to the doctrines and precepts of Christ."

In so far, they are separated from the world, set apart to become holy, consecrated to Christ. Not that their sanctification or saintship is complete. If that were the case, the apostles would not have written epistles to the saints. For perfect beings need no Bibles, no Churches, no means of Grace. The angels need none of these things. There is not one sinless person mentioned in the Bible, except that divine One, "who committed no sin, neither was guile found in His mouth"(1 Peter 2:22). If there were one Scripture character who, if such a thing were possible, would have attained to sinless perfection, that one would certainly have been the greatest of all the apostles. He labored more than they all; he suffered more than they all; he went deeper into the mysteries of redemption than they all. He was not only permitted to look into heaven, as the beloved John, but he "was caught up into paradise—whether in the body or out of the body I do not know, God knows— and he heard things that cannot be told, which man may not utter"(2 Corinthians 12:3-4) on this sinful earth. Oh, what purifying sinless perfection. Indeed, he never ceased to mourn and lament the sinfulness and imperfection of his own heart, and called himself the chief of sinners.

He does indeed speak of perfection. Hear what he says, Philippians 3:12—14:

Not that I have already obtained this or am already perfect, but I press on to make it my own, because Christ Jesus has made me his own. Brothers, I do not consider that I have made it my own. But one thing I do: forgetting what lies behind and straining forward to what lies ahead, I press on toward the goal for the prize of the upward call of God in Christ Jesus.

The saints on earth, then, are not sinless ones. The Bible does indeed speak of those born of God not committing sin. But this can only mean that they do not willfully sin. They do not intentionally live in habits of sin. Their sins are sins of weakness and not sins of malice. They repent of them, mourn over them, and strive against them. They constantly pray, "Forgive us our trespasses as we forgive those who trespass against us." Their heart-purity and sanctification are only relative. Sanctification is gradual and progressive.

We have seen that Paul thus expressed himself. He was constantly "following after," "reaching forth," "pressing toward" the mark. He exhorts the Corinthians, 2 Corinthians 7:1, to be "bringing holiness to completion in the fear of God," and again, 2 Corinthians 3:18, to be "transformed into the same image from glory to glory." He tells them in chapter 4:16 that, "the inward self is renewed day by day." He exhorts the saints or believers, again and again "to grow," "to increase," "to abound yet more and more." Growth is the law of the kingdom of nature. And the same God operates in the kingdom of Grace, and, indeed, much after the same order.

Our Savior, therefore, so often compares the kingdom of God, or the kingdom of Grace, to growth from a seed, where it is "first the blade, then the ear, then the full grain in the ear" Mark 4:26-29. In harmony with all this, Paul calls those who have lately become believers, the "infants in Christ"(1 Corinthians 3:1) to grow in Grace and in knowledge. How directly contrary to all this is the unscriptural idea, not only of entire sanctification, but of instantaneous sanctification. Surely, in this fast age, many have run far ahead of prophets, apostles, martyrs, reformers and the most eminent saints of all ages. As we read the lives and words of these heroes of faith, we find that the more Christ-like and consecrated they were, the more did they deplore their slow progress and their remaining sin.

While, therefore, we have no Scripture warrant to expect sinlessness here; while we must "die daily,"(1 Corinthians 15:31) "mortify our members"(Colossians 3:5) and "fight the good fight of faith,"(1 Timothy 6:12) between the old Adam, whose remnants cleave to us, and the new man in Christ Jesus, we can still do much to promote our sanctification, and make it more and more complete. We can use the powers that God has given us to carry on the warfare with sin. We can increase these powers, or rather permit divine Grace to increase them, by a diligent use of the means of Grace. In the chapter on the Word of God as a means of Grace, we showed that the Holy Spirit sanctifies through the Word. In the chapters on baptism and the baptismal covenant, we showed how that holy sacrament is a means of Grace, whose efficacy is not confined to the time of its administration, but that it is intended to be a perennial fountain of Grace, from which we can drink and be refreshed while life lasts. That for our daily life it means that:

The old Adam in us is to be drowned and destroyed by daily sorrow and repentance together with all sins and evil lusts and that the new man should daily come forth and rise and shall live in the presence of God in righteousness and purity forever.

In the chapters on the Lord's Supper, we learned that it also was ordained and instituted to sustain and strengthen our spiritual life.

We have, therefore, all the means necessary for our sanctification. Do we prayerfully use them? Might we not be much further on in the work of holiness than we are? Do we use the truth as we should, that we may be "sanctified by the truth?"(John 17:17). Do we "long for the pure spiritual milk, that by it we may grow up into salvation?"(1 Peter 2:2). Does it "dwell richly among us?"(Colossians 3:16). Do we know that "as many of us as were baptized were baptized into His death?"(Romans 6:3). Do we say, with those early Christians, "From now on let no one cause me trouble, for I bear on my body the marks of Jesus"(Galatians 6:17). And when we go to our Lord's Table do we realize that His "flesh is true food, and His blood is true drink?"(John 6:55). Do we go in the strength of that heavenly nourishment many days? Might we not, by making a more sincere, hearty and diligent use of all these means of Grace, live nearer to Christ, lean more confidingly on Him and do more effectually all things through Him who strengthened us?

Yes, without a doubt, we must all confess that it is our own fault that we are not sanctified more fully than we are; that if, in the strength derived from a proper use of the means of Grace, we would watch more over self, pray more, meditate more on divine things and thus surround ourselves more with a spiritual atmosphere, we should be more spiritual. "This is the will of

SANCTIFICATION

God, your sanctification"(1 Thessalonians 4:3). "Without holiness, no man shall see the Lord" (Hebrews 12:14).

And what am I? My soul, awake,
And an impartial surrey take.
Does no dark sign, no ground of fear
In practice or in heart appear?
What Image does my spirit bear?
Is Jesus formed and living there?
Ah, do His lineaments divine
In thought and word and action shine?
Searcher of hearts, O search me still.
The secrets of my soul reveal;
My fears remove; let me appear
To God and my own conscience clear.

23

Revivals

WE might have closed our studies of the Way of Salvation with Sanctification, without giving any attention to the subject of Revivals. We remember, however, that, in the estimation of many, revivals are the most essential part of the Way; so much so that, in certain quarters, few, if any, souls are expected to be brought into the way of life, otherwise than through so-called "revivals of religion." According to this wide spread idea, the ingathering of souls, the building up of the Church, her activity, power and very life, are dependent upon the revival system. In view of all this, we have concluded to bring our studies to a close with an examination of this system.

Before we enter upon the subject itself, however, we desire to have it distinctly understood that we intend to discuss the system, and not the people who believe and practice it. There is no doubt that there are great Christian people who have a religion dependent on such movements, and there may be very unchristian people who oppose this system. We have nothing to do with this. We are not discussing persons, but doctrines and systems. The advocates of modern revivalism claim the right to hold, defend and propagate their views. We only demand the same right. If we do not favor or practice their way, our people have not only a right to ask for, but it is our duty to give the grounds and reasons for our position.

In discussing this subject, we intend, as usual, to speak with all candor and plainness. We desire to approach and view this subject, as every subject, from the fair, firm standpoint of the opening words of the Formula of Con cord, viz.:

We believe, teach and confess that the only rule and standard, according to which all doctrines and teachings should be esteemed and judged, are nothing else than the prophetic and apostolic Scriptures of the Old and New Testament.

We wish to test it by the infallible Word. By it, we are willing to be judged. According to it, our doctrines and practices must stand or fall. What then is a revival? The word "revive" means to bring back to life. It presupposes the existence of life, which for a time had languished or died. Life was present, it failed and was restored. Strictly speaking, therefore, we can only use this word of the bringing back of a life that had once been there but was lost. Applying it to spiritual life, strictly speaking, only a person who has once had the new life in him, but lost it for a while and regained it, can be said to be revived. So, likewise, only a church or a community that was once spiritually alive, but had grown languid and lifeless, can be said to be revived.

On the other hand, it is an improper use of terms to apply the word revival to the work of a foreign missionary, who for the first time preaches the life-giving Word, and through it gathers converts and organizes Churches. In his case it is a first enkindling and not a restoring, of life. All those Old Testament reformations and restorations to the true worship and service of the true God, after a time of decline and apostasy, were revivals according to the strict sense of the word. For these revivals patriarchs and prophets labored and prayed. On the other hand, the labors and successes of the apostles in the New Testament were not strictly revivals. They preached the Gospel instead of the law. They preached a Redeemer who had come, instead of one who was to come.

It was largely a new faith, a new life, a new way of life that they taught, and in so far a new Church that they established. Its types, shadows and roots, had all been in the old Covenant and Church. But so different were the fulfillments from the promises, that it was truly called a New Dispensation. And, therefore, the labors of the apostles to establish this dispensation were largely missionary labors. It was not so much the restoring of an old faith and life, as the bringing in of a new. We find their parallel in foreign mission work much more than in regular Church work. It is by overlooking this distinction that many erroneous doctrines and practices have crept into the Church, e. g., as to infant baptism, conversion and modern revivalism.

As to revivals, popularly so-called, we maintain, first of all, that it ought to be the policy and aim of the Church to preclude their necessity. It is generally admitted that they are only needed, longed for and obtained, after a period of spiritual decline and general worldliness. A Church that is alive and active needs no revival. A lifeless Church does. Better then, far better, use every right endeavor to keep the Church alive and active, than permit it to grow cold and worldly, with a view and hope of a glorious awakening. Prevention is better than cure. We should rather pay a family physician to prevent disease and keep us well, than to employ even the most distinguished doctor to cure a sick household; especially so if the probability were that, in some cases, the healing would be only partial, and in others it would eventuate in an aggravation of the disease.

In the chapters on the Baptismal Covenant and Conversion, we showed that it is possible to keep that covenant and thus always grow in Grace and in the knowledge of our Lord Jesus Christ. While we sorrowfully admitted that the cases of such as do this are not as numerous as is possible and most desirable, we also learned that they might be far more numerous, if parents and teachers understood their responsibility and did their duty to the baptized children. We verily believe that thus it might become the rule, instead of the exception, that the children of Christian parents should grow up as Christ's lambs from baptism, should love Him with their earliest love and never wander into the ways of willful sin. We also firmly believe that those who were thus early consecrated, trained, taught and nurtured in faith and love, make the healthiest, the strongest and most reliable members and workers in the Church. Neither can we for a moment doubt that such is the good and gracious will of Him who desires the little children to be baptized into Him.

It certainly seems repugnant to all that we have ever learned of our God and Savior, that it should be His will that our dear children, who have been conceived and born in sin, and are therefore by nature, or by birth, the children of wrath, should remain in this state of sin and condemnation until they are old enough to be converted at a revival. Yet it must be either that, or a denial of the Bible doctrine of original sin, if we accept the teachings and practices of modern revivalism. We are not prepared for either of these positions. Therefore it is our great aim and object to recall the Church to the old paths. Therefore we are concerned to see the Church firmly established on the old foundations of the doctrine of original sin, of baptism for the remission of sins, of training up in that baptismal covenant by the constant, diligent and persevering teaching of God's Word, in the family, in the Sunday School, in the catechetical class and from the pulpit. In proportion as all this is accomplished, in that proportion will we preclude the necessity of conversions and, consequently, of revivals.

Who will say that a congregation made up of such as are "sanctified from the womb," "lent to the Lord" from birth, having "known the Holy Scripture" from childhood, would not be a healthy, living Church? Such a Church would need no revival. Would it be possible to have such a Church? Is it possible for any one member to grow up and remain a child of God? If possible for one, why not for a whole congregation? Are the means of Grace inadequate? No, no! The whole trouble lies in the neglect or abuse of the means. With their proper use, the whole aspect of religious life might be different from what it is. It is not a fatal necessity that one, or more, or all the members of a church must periodically grow cold, lose their first love, and backslide from their God. It is not God's will, but their fault, that it should be so.

While the church at Ephesus lost its first love, and that at Pergamos permitted false doctrine to creep into it and be a stumbling block, and that at Thyatira suffered Jezebel to seduce Christ's servants, and that at Sardis did not have her works found perfect before God, and that of Laodicea had become luke warm; yet the church at Smyrna, with all her tribulation and poverty and persecution, remained rich and faithful in the sight of God, and that at Philadelphia had kept the Word of God's patience, and her enemies were to know that God loved her. While the former five were censured, the latter two were approved. The former might have remained as faithful as the latter. It was their own fault and sin that the former needed a revival. The latter needed none. Which were the better off! We believe that where there is a sound, faithful and earnest pastor, and a docile, sincere, earnest, united and active people, many will grow up in their baptismal covenant; and among those who wander more or less there from, there will be frequent conversions, under the faithful use of the ordinary services and ordinances of the Church. Such, we believe, were the pastorates of Richard Baxter, at Kidderminster; of Ludwig Harms, at Hermans- burg; of Oberlin, at Steinthal; and of our late lamented Dr. Greenwald, at Easton and Lancaster. None of these churches, after their pastors were fairly established in them, needed so called revivals. And such, doubtless, have been thousands of quiet, faithful pastorates, some known to the world, and others known only to God. Blessed are those churches in which the work of Grace is constantly and effectively going on, according to God's Way of Salvation.

24

Modern Revivals

WE have shown that it ought to be the great aim and object of the Church to preclude the necessity of occasional religious excitements. We also showed, by example from Scripture and from Church history, that it is possible to attain to this end. If parents did but understand and do their whole duty in the family, teachers in the Sunday-school and pastors in the catechetical class, in the pulpit and from house to house, children would very generally grow up in their baptismal covenant; and a church made up of such members would not depend for its growth and life on periodic religious revivals. But—alas that "but!"—parents, teachers and pastors too often come short of their duty. Carelessness, worldliness and godlessness hold sway in too many of the congregations, homes and families. There is a love of pleasure, a greed for gain and a haste to be rich, that has taken hold of the heart and life of too many professedly Christian parents.

There is no time for God's Word or earnest prayer with and for the children. There is often little if any religious instruction or Christian example. The little ones breathe in a withering, poisonous, materialistic atmosphere. The germs of the divine life, implanted in baptism, either lie dormant, or are blighted after their first manifestations. They grow up with the idea that the great object of life is to gain the most, and make the best of this world. Oh, how much is wrong in many of the homes and families of our people! Bad home life is responsible for the downfall of thousands of our children and young people. Countless drunkards, gamblers, foul-mouthed and profane wretches, brutes, bad women, criminals and fiends in human form once sat on a mother's lap and were pressed to her bosom. Has there not been a terrible letting down of the moral and spiritual life of the home? Thousands of children are growing up in Godless and Christless homes. The Word, the prayer, the spiritual impression and guidance so much needed are not there. In all too many homes there are card and pool tables, swearing victrolas, debasing and irreverent books and papers, bad example and bad company. The only god that is extolled, followed and sacrificed to is the god of pleasure or the god of wealth.

From such homes the children go out into the world that lies in wickedness. The boys, unguided, soon get into the wrong gangs and the girls into bad sets. Their souls can be corrupted by keeping such companions. Virtue soon becomes cheap and is easily lost. The debasing moving picture show, with its gilding of crime, it's heroizing of criminals, its laughing at the unspeakable tragedy of a woman's loss of virtue, its coarse and brutalizing scenes of drinking and debauchery continue the ruin of childhood and youth. Conscience becomes more and more deadened until its voice is no longer heard. Is it any wonder that there is an appalling increase of vice and crime among the young? And so many of these come from the families of our Church and Sunday School people. So many have been instructed and confirmed. Did the Sunday School teachers do their part? Alas, they have in many cases been all too careless and trifling. They do not live close to Christ themselves, and how can they lead their pupils nearer to Him? They scarcely pray for themselves, much less for their pupils, and how can they instill into them a spirit of prayer? And what of the pastors? Have they been as earnest and consecrated as they should be? We fear that too many are not burning with a desire for souls. They go through their ministerial duties in a formal, lifeless manner, and their labors are barren of results.

When such pastors look upon these lapsed and lost ones can they say that they have done their part? Did they instruct, warn and beseech parents and young people day and night with tears? Can they say with Paul: "I am clean of the blood of all" these? Is not an awakening needed? Should there not be a special evangelistic campaign? Was not Doctor Jacobs right when he reported to the General Council in Bock Island:

In view of the godless spirit of the age, the floods of wickedness in high places and in low and the currents of ungodliness and indifference that enter the Church with their deadening and paralyzing effects even upon many entrusted with the holy office of the ministry; in a time and land where the cardinal doctrines of Christianity are constantly assailed both openly and perhaps, even more dangerously by the ignoring of Christian standards in our schools and literature — especially in the public press; and Amidst widespread demands that the Church shall be restricted to the sphere of a purely ethical and social institution and that the great verities of our Holy Faith and God's Word be consigned to obscurity; we appreciate the efforts of earnest men to awaken a lost world and a sleeping Church to the great realities of God and eternity, of sin and redemption and rejoice in every success gained in the winning of men to Christ and the stemming to any degree of the tide of materialism and false spiritualism around us.

If then we admit that times of refreshing are often needed, why not have them after the manner of those around us? Why not adopt the modern system, have union meetings, evangelists, high-pressure methods, excitements, the anxious bench, the saw-dust trail, the magnetic hand-shake, and all the modern machinery for getting up revivals? We will briefly state our objections to this system.

First, we object to the modern revival system, because it rests on an entire misconception of the coming and work of the Holy Spirit. The idea seems to be that the Holy Spirit is not effectively present in the regular and ordinary services of the sanctuary; that He came to the Church as a transient guest on the day of Pentecost, then departed again, and returned when there was another season of special interest. That He then left again, and ever since has come and worked with power during every revival, and then departed to be absent until the next. We claim that this is directly contrary to the teaching of the Divine Word.

When Jesus was about to leave His disciples they were filled with deep sorrow. He gathered them around Him, in that upper chamber at Jerusalem, and comforted them in those tender, loving words, recorded in the fourteenth, fifteenth and sixteenth chapters of John. In these chapters He promises and speaks much of a Comforter, whom He would send. The whole discourse goes to show that this Comforter was intended to be substituted for the visible presence of Himself. His own visible presence was to be withdrawn. The Comforter was to be sent to take His place, and thus, in a manner, make good the loss. Jesus had been their comforter and their joy. They would no longer have Him visibly among them, to walk with Him, to talk with Him, to hear the life-giving words that fell from His lips. The announcement made them feel as if they were to be left "comfortless" and forsaken. But he says, John 14:16-18:

And I will ask the Father, and he will give you another Helper to be with you forever, even the Spirit of truth, whom the world cannot receive, because it neither sees him nor knows him. You know him, for he dwells with you and will be in you. I will not leave you as orphans; I will come to you.

And in John 16:

But now I am going to him who sent me, and none of you asks me, 'Where are you going?' But because I have said these things to you, sorrow has filled your heart. Nevertheless, I tell you the truth: it is to your advantage that I go away, for if I do not go away, the Helper will not come to you. But if I go, I will send him to you (John 16:5-7).

From these words, and others in these chapters, two things are plain: First, that the Comforter came as the visible Christ's substitute; Secondly, that He came to abide. While Jesus was to be absent, as far as His visible presence was concerned, the divine Comforter, the Holy Spirit, was to take His place. His presence was to substitute the visible Christ. But if He had come to be present only briefly, and occasionally, after long intervals of absence, it would be a poor filling of the painful void. Evidently the impression designed to be made by the words of Jesus was, that the Holy Spirit would come to abide. And this is made still more clear by the plain words of Jesus quoted above "I will not leave you orphans;" "He shall abide with you forever." He came, then, as a substitute; He came also to abide forever. The revival system is, however, built up on the idea that He comes and goes. He visits the Church, and leaves it again. At so-called revival seasons the Church has a Comforter. During all the rest of the time she is left in a desolate or orphaned state. Thus is the revival system built up on an entire misconception and misapprehension as to the coming and abiding of the Holy Spirit.

It likewise misconceives entirely the operations of the Spirit. The idea seems to be that this Blessed One operates without means, directly, arbitrarily and at haphazard. The Word and Sacraments are not duly recognized as the divinely ordained means and channels, through which He reaches the hearts of the children of men. That this is an unscriptural idea we have shown elsewhere. That the Spirit uses the means of grace as channels and instruments, through which He comes and operates on the hearts of men and imparts to them renewing and sanctifying grace, is taught all through the New Testament. We need not enlarge on these points again, but refer our readers to what has been written above on this subject.

Our second objection to the modern revival system arises out of the first. Because of the errors concerning the coming and the operations of the Holy Spirit, the system under values the divinely-ordained means of Grace. Little if any renewing Grace is expected from the sacrament of Christian Baptism. Few if any conversions are expected from the regular and ordinary preaching of the Word. Little if any spiritual nourishment is expected from the sacrament of the Lord's Supper. Who that has studied such meetings has not heard the idea of Grace bestowed through Baptism ridiculed? Who has not heard so-called revival preachers scout the idea of "getting religion" — which must mean receiving divine Grace if it means anything — through catechizing the young in the doctrines of the divine Word? Aren't these divine means often entirely set aside by the most enthusiastic revivalists? Who does not know that often at these revival services the reading and sometimes the preaching of the Word are entirely omitted? Thus God's means, the means used by Christ and His apostles, are undervalued. They are used at the ordinary services, when there is no revival going on, but not much is expected of them.

Our third objection arises from the second. Because the regular Church oridinances are undervalued, they are largely fruitless. Because people do not have much faith in their efficacy, they do not receive much benefit from them. Few conversions are expected or reported during the ten or eleven months of regular or ordinary church services, while many, if not all, are expected and reported from the few weeks of special effort. Even the work of sanctification is largely crowded into the few weeks. It is during these few weeks that saints expect to be quickened, refreshed, strengthened and purified, more than during all the rest of the year. It is doubtless both as a cause and a result of this undervaluing and general fruitlessness of the ordinary Church ordinances, that we find so much levity and irreverence in many so- called revival Churches. Because the Holy Spirit is not supposed to be effectively present, is not in the Word and Sacraments, does not bring His saving and sanctifying grace through them; therefore there is nothing solemn, awe-inspiring, or uplifting in these things. Therefore the young, and sometimes older ones, go to these churches as to places of amusement, to have a good time, to laugh, to whisper, to gaze about, write notes, get company, and what not. A careful observer cannot fail to notice that in Churches which believe in and preach Grace through the means of Grace, there is an atmosphere of deeper solemnity and more earnest devotion than in such revival Churches. The above objection to the revival system we believe will explain the difference.

We object fourthly to the so-called revival system because, as a natural result of the above, it begets a dependence on something extraordinary and miraculous for bringing sinners into the kingdom. As we have seen, these Churches expect nearly all their conversions from "revivals." It naturally follows that the unconverted will shake off and get rid of all serious thoughts and impressions at the regular church services, under the plea that they will give this matter their attention when the next revival comes round. We have more than once heard persons say, in effect, "Oh well, I know I'm not what I ought to be, but perhaps I'll be converted at the next revival." Thus the gracious influences of the blessed Spirit, as they come through the Word, whether from the pulpit, the Sunday-school teacher, or Christian friend, or even when that Word is brought to a funeral or sick-bed, are all put aside with the hope that there may be a change at the next revival. And we verily believe that such ideas, fostered by a false system, have kept countless souls out of the kingdom of God.

We object fifthly that at these so-called revivals there is a dependence on methods not sanctioned or authorized by the Word of God. As we have seen, God's means are generally slighted. On the other hand, human means and methods are exalted and magnified. The anxious bench is regarded by many otherwise sensible people, as a veritable mercy seat, where Grace is supposed to abound — as though the Spirit of God manifested His saving and sanctifying power there as nowhere else. But this is a purely human institution, and has no warrant in the Word. On this point it is not necessary to enlarge.

25

Modern Revivals (Part 2)

WE continue our objections to the modern revival system. Our sixth objection is the utter indifference to doctrine that generally goes hand in hand with its methods and practices. To "contend for the faith that was once delivered to the saints,"(Jude 3) seems to be altogether out of place at a modern revival. There is no "keeping a close watch on your teaching,"(1 Timothy 4:16) or "following the pattern of sound words,"(2 Timothy 1:13) or "becoming rooted and built up in Christ, and established in the faith just as you were taught"(Colossians 2:7). There is no counseling to "no longer be children, tossed to and fro by the waves and carried about with every wind of doctrine"(Ephesians 4:14) no warning against false teachers and false doctrines. Instead of thus following Christ and His Apostles, in insisting on the truth, the faith, and the doctrine; instead of thus warning against error or false doctrine, and showing that it "spreads like gangrene"(2 Timothy 2:17) and endanger the very salvation of the soul, the modern revival system habitually inveighs against all such loyalty to the truth and contending for the faith and pure doctrine as bigotry, intolerance, lack of charity, if not lack of all "experimental religion."

In many quarters indeed the idea is boldly advanced that the more a person stands up for pure doctrine, for Word and Sacrament as channels of Grace, the less Grace he has; and the more he makes light of doctrine, the less positive conviction he has; the less he thinks of creeds, catechism, and confessions of faith, the more religion he has! The popular sentiment is: it makes no difference what a person believes, or to what Church he belongs, or indeed, whether he belongs to any, if only he is converted; if only he means well; if only the heart is right! Now, it is not necessary to show here again that all such indifference to doctrine is directly contrary to the teaching of Christ and His apostles.

Our seventh objection is closely connected with the last. Where there is so much indifference to the Truth as it is in Jesus, that it often amounts to open contempt, we cannot expect any provision for teaching His saving truths to men. Hence we find but small provision, if any, for doctrinal instruction in the revival system. Those who are expected to be gathered in, converted and brought to Christ, are not instructed first. They do not learn what sin is, what Grace is, and how it is communicated and applied. They are left in ignorance of the great doctrines of sin and salvation. They have the most imperfect conception of God's Way of Salvation. And yet they are expected to enter upon that way, and walk in it. They are exhorted to be converted, to get religion, and to believe, while it is seldom, if ever, made clear what all this means, and how it is brought about. Surely it is not necessary that we should show that if ever a person needs to act intelligently — if ever he needs to know exactly what he is doing, why he is doing it, and what is involved in so doing — it is when he is acting in the interests of his eternal salvation. Then, if ever, he should act understandingly and honestly. And for this he needs instruction. We have shown elsewhere that this is God's way, the Bible way, the way of the early Church, the way of the great Protestant Reformation, and the way of our Church of the Reformation to this day. We therefore object to this modern revival system, because it has largely supplanted the old time systematic and thorough indoctrination of the young. And, as we have elsewhere said, we are convinced that, just in proportion as the youth are un-catechized and uninstructed in the great doctrines of God's Word regarding sin and grace, in that proportion will doubt, skepticism, unbelief and infidelity infect them, and lead them into the paths of the destroyer.

Our eighth objection to this modern revival system is that it is so largely built up on the excitement of the feelings. The first and great object of the revivalist seems to be to work directly on the emotional nature of his hearers. If he can stir the depths of the heart until it throbs and thrills with pent-up emotions, if he can play upon its chords until they vibrate and tremble under his touch, until its hidden chambers ring again with responsive longings until at last the repressed intensity breaks forth in overpowering excitement, he is considered a successful revival preacher. To reach this end the preaching is made up of exhortations, anecdotes and appeals. There are touching stories, calculated to make the tender hearted weep. There are thrilling and startling experiences, calculated to frighten the more hard-hearted. There are lively, emotional songs, with stirring music, calculated to affect the nervous system and bring about strange sensations. And when the feelings are aroused, when the excitement is up, the hearers are urged to come forward, to go to the inquiry room, to stand up, to follow the saw-dust trail and shake hands with the evangelist, or to do something else to show that they are ready to take the decisive step.

Now, as we have shown above, if ever a person needs to be calm and deliberate, it is when about to take the most important step of his whole life. But men do not generally take important steps, or enter upon decisive movements, when they are excited. When one is excited he is very apt to do the wrong thing, and to regret it afterwards. Not that we object to all feeling in religion. We by no means believe in a religion without feeling. We know of no true piety without deep and heartfelt sorrow for sin, and earnest longings for ever closer union and fellowship with God, together with a childlike trust and a fervent love to Him. We believe, however, that the heart, with its emotions, can only be effectively reached through the understanding. Through the mind we work on the heart. Through the judgment we change the feelings. We appeal first to the intellect, to instruct, to enlighten, to give clear and correct views and ideas, then through the intellect to the heart.

When Paul was sent to convert the Gentiles, his direction was first of all "to open their eyes" — that is, to instruct them — and then to "turn them from darkness to light." Paul was not to begin on the feelings, but on the intellect. But the modern revival system reverses this method. It makes a short cut, and goes at once to the feelings, without first enlightening the mind. This is contrary, not only to the Scriptures, but it is also directly contrary to the science and laws of the mind. It contradicts true psychology and true theology as well as the Bible. We believe that where there is the proper instruction in the great saving doctrines of God's Word, where the mind is properly enlightened to know what sin is, what salvation is, and how it is obtained, there, unless there is a positive and determined resistance to the power of truth, the proper feelings will come of their own accord. It will require no heart rending stories, no frantic appeals, no violent exhortations to bring them about. But we object to the revival system, because it is almost entirely built up on feeling, and thus reaches only one department of man's complex nature. Instead of changing the whole immaterial man— his intellect, his sensibilities, and his will—it spends its force on the insensibilities alone.

Our ninth objection we can state briefly. Because the revival system undervalues sound doctrine and instruction therein, and because it depends so largely on feeling, it not only permits but encourages the ignorant and inexperienced to assist in exhorting and helping those who are inquiring after life and salvation. Those who have scarcely "got through" themselves, who have given little earnest study to God's Way of Salvation, who do not know the alphabet of Grace, and the means and methods of Grace,—these are often the pretended instructors at the anxious bench and in the meetings for inquirers. Now, we object strongly to such procedures. "Can a blind man lead a blind man? Will they not both fall into the pit?"(Luke 6:39). Better let these novices themselves sit at the feet of Christ. Let Christ's authorized teachers instruct them in God's Way of Salvation, before they undertake to lead other lost and groping ones.

We object finally that, at the experience and testimony meetings, held in connection with modern revivals, not only novices, as described above, but those who have been the worst sinners, are encouraged to speak, and are at least permitted to recount and seemingly to glory in their former sins. They do not speak as Paul did, when compelled to refer to his former life, with deep sorrow and shame, but often jestingly, flippantly, and as if they imagined that they ought now to be looked upon and admired as great heroes. We believe that this is all wrong and productive of great harm. The unconverted youth, listening to such talk, says to himself, "Well, if such a person can so suddenly rise and be looked up to and be made a teacher of others, a leader of the experience and prayer-meeting, certainly I need not be uneasy; for I have a long way to go, before I get as far as he was." Therefore, we object to all such conduct. It is not only unscriptural, but unbecoming. It is an offense against good breeding and common decency. It does great harm.

But enough. We might still speak of the spirit of self-righteousness engendered and fostered by this system. We might speak of the sad results that follow with so many — how that persons become excited, have strange sensations and feelings, imagine that this is religion, afterwards find that they have the same old heart, no strength against sin, no peace of conscience, none of that bliss and joy they heard others speak of and expected for themselves, and how they gradually fall back into their old mode of life, become harder than ever, and at last drift into hopeless unbelief, and say: "There is nothing in religion; I've tried it, and found it a delusion." Thus is their last state worse than their first. We might show that in sections of country where this false system has held sway, worldliness and skepticism abound. These places have been aptly called "burnt districts." It seems next to impossible to make lasting impressions for good on such communities. We might speak of the proselyting spirit that so often accompanies this system.

How with all its protestations of charity, brotherly love, and union, it often runs out into the meanest spirit of casting aspersions on others and stealing from their churches. We might speak of the divided churches that often result. As Dr. Krauth once forcibly said, "They are united to pieces, and revived to death." We might point to the divided households, to the destruction of family peace, to the many sad heart-burnings and alienations that result. But we forbear. The whole system is an invention of man. It is unscriptural from beginning to end. We cannot conceive of our blessed Savior or of His apostles conducting a modern revival. The mind revolts at the idea.

26

Modern Revivals (Part 3)

WE have given a number of reasons for refusing to favor or adopt the modern revival system as a part of the Way of Salvation. We now add the testimony of others, not only of our own communion, but also of other denominations. Undoubtedly one of the greatest and most important of these religious movements was that one which swept over Presbyterian and Congregational Churches of New England, New Jersey, Pennsylvania, and Virginia, about the middle of the eighteenth century. It is generally known and spoken of as "the great awakening." Its leading spirits were such staunch and loyal Calvinists as Jonathan Edwards, the Tennents, Blair, and others. In the matter of doctrinal preaching and instruction it was certainly very far in advance of the so-called revivals of the present day. And yet in many of its direct results it was anything but salutary. It was the principal cause of the division of the Presbyterian Church into Old and New School. Let us hear what some of the eminent theologians of these Churches say of the results of "the great awakening."

Dr. Sereno E. Dwight, the biographer of Jonathan Edwards, and one of his descendants says:

It is deserving perhaps of inquiry, whether the subsequent slumbers of the American Church for nearly seventy years may not be ascribed, in an important degree, to the fatal reaction of these unhappy measures.

Jonathan Edwards, himself the most zealous and successful promoter of the whole movement, in 1750, when its fruits could be fairly tested, writes thus:

Multitudes of fair and high professors, in one place and another, have sadly backslidden; sinners are desperately hardened; experimental religion is more than ever out of credit with the far greater part, and the doctrines of Grace and those principles in religion that do chiefly concern the power of godliness are far more than ever discarded. Arminianism and Pelagianism have made strange progress within a few years… Many professors are gone off to great lengths in enthusiasm and extravagance in their notions and practices. Great contentions, separations, and confusions in our religious state prevail in many parts of the land.

The above is from a letter to a friend in Scotland. We give also a brief quotation from his farewell sermon to his church at Nottingham:

Another thing that vastly concerns your future prosperity is that you should watch against the encroachments of error, and particularly Arminianism and doctrines of like tendency…These doctrines at this day are much more prevalent than they were formerly. The progress they have made in the land within this seven years (i.e. since the revival), seems to have been vastly greater than at any time in the like space before. And they are still prevailing and creeping into almost all parts of the land, threatening the utter ruin of the credit of those doctrines which are the peculiar glory of the Gospel and the interests of vital piety.

Dr. Van Rensselaer, in commenting on these and other serious words of the great Jonathan Edwards, says:

And what was the final result? Arminianism led the way to Socinianism, and near the beginning of the nineteenth century there was but a single orthodox Congregational church in Boston. Harvard University had lapsed into heresy, and about a third of the churches of the Puritans denied the faith held by their fathers.

And all this he traces back to that "great awakening." He further says:

A work so great and extensive was accompanied by incidents which made many good men doubtful as to its effects on the Church. Special seasons of religious interest are seasons of danger and temptation even under the guidance of the most enlightened and prudent...Good men differ much in their estimate of the awakening, and the fruits of the work in many places afforded reason of much apprehension... In its earlier stages the revival was unquestionably the occasion of the confession of many souls. It was like one of those mighty rains of summer which refresh many a plant and tree, but which are accompanied, in many places, with hail and storm and overflowing desolation, and which are followed by a long, dreary drought. The Presbyterian Church welcomes fair revivals, sent by the Holy Spirit, but is averse to man-made schemes for getting up temporary excitements which have been so prevalent in our day.

During the years between 1830-1850, another revival agitation swept over the American Church. It was during this time, especially, that our English Lutheran churches caught the contagion, introduced the "new measures," such as the "mourner's bench," "protracted meetings," the admission of members without catechetical instruction, and many other novelties. In not a few places, so-called Lutherans vied with the most fanatical sects in their wild extravagances.

Those who adhered to the time-honored method and spirit of conservative Lutheranism, who preached the Word in all its simplicity, catechized the young, taught that the Spirit and Grace of God can only be expected to operate through Christ's own means, through Word and Sacrament, were denounced as formalists, who knew nothing of vital piety. Among the leading advocates of the new way was the Rev. Reuben Weiser. This now departed brother, with many other serious and thoughtful men, afterwards saw the error of his ways, and frankly and publicly confessed his change of conviction in the Lutheran Observer. He says:

In 1842 Dr. J. W. Nevin, of the German Reformed Church, published a pamphlet called 'The Anxious Bench.' It was, for that time, a bold and vigorous arraignment of the whole modern revival system. He warned the German churches against this style of religion, but his warning was not much heeded at the time. I felt it my duty to reply to Dr. Nevin in a pamphlet called 'The Mourners' Bench.' At that time I was in the midst of the most extensive revival of my whole ministry. I was honest and sincere in my views, for I had not seen then many of the evils that were almost certain to follow in the wake of revivals as they were then conducted. Personally, I respected and esteemed Dr. Nevin highly, but as he had opposed my cherished views, I felt it my duty to write against him. I said some things long since regretted, and now, after the lapse of nearly half a century, make this amend honorable. And it must be a source of pleasure to Dr. Nevin, who is still living, that the views which he so ably advocated in the face of much bitter opposition have been generally adopted by nearly all the Churches.

Dr. Weiser proceeds:

Many of our churches that fostered this system were in the end injured by it…Under the revival system it was very natural for the people to become dissatisfied with the ordinary means of Grace. There was a constant longing for excitement, and when the ebullition of feeling abated, many thought they had 'lost their religion.' The next move was that as the preacher was so dead and lifeless they must get another who had more fire, and thus the old pastor was sent adrift.

Elsewhere Dr. Weiser has clearly expressed himself as having become firmly convinced that the old churchly method of careful and systematic catechizing of the young, is the only sure and safe way of building up the Church. He also quotes Dr. Morris as saying:

The 'mourner's bench' was introduced into Lutheran churches in imitation of the Methodists, and also disorders, such as shouting, clapping of hands, groaning, and singing of choruses of doggerel verses to the most frivolous tunes, whilst ministers or members, and sometimes women, were engaged in speaking to the mourners. Feelings were aroused, as usual, by portraying the horrors of hell, reciting affecting stories, alluding to deaths in families, violent vociferation, and other means. At prayer often all would pray as loud as the leader. These exercises would continue night after night, until the physical energies were exhausted.

Dr. H. E. Jacobs, in his preface to Rev. G. H. Trabert's tract on "Genuine versus Spurious Revivals," writes thus of the system:

This system, if system it may be called, is in many of its elements simply a reproduction of the Romish errors against which our fathers bore testimony in the days of the Reformation. Wide as is the apparent difference, we find in both the same corruption of the doctrine of justification by faith alone without works, the same ignoring of the depths of natural depravity, the same exaltation of human strength and merit, the same figment of human preparation for God's Grace, the same confounding of the fruits of faith with the conditions of faith, the same aversion to the careful study of God's Word, the same indifference to sound doctrine, and the same substitution of subjective frames of mind and forms of experience for the great objective facts of Christianity, as the grounds of God's favor.

In both cases, all spiritual strength, which is inseparable from complete dependence solely upon the Word and promise of God, and not in any way upon human sensations and preparations, is either withheld, destroyed, or greatly hindered; and uncertainty and vacillation, despair, infidelity and ruin, often end the sad story of those who are thus left without any firm support amidst the trials of life, and under the strokes of God's judgments.

The same Church which in the days of the Reformation raised her voice against these errors, when she found the entire life of Christianity endangered by them, can be silent in the present hour, when the same errors appear all around her, only by betraying her trust, and incurring the guilt of the faithless watchman who fails to give alarm.

Let us hear also the testimony of our late lamented Dr. Krauth. He says, as quoted by Rev. Trabert:

How often are the urging that we are all one, the holding of union meetings, the effusive rapture of all-forgiving, all-forgetting, all-embracing love, the preliminary to the meanest sectarian tricks, dividing congregations, tearing families to pieces, and luring away the unstable. The short millennium of such love is followed by the fresh loosing of the Satan of malevolence out of his prison, and the clashing in battle of the Gog and Magog of sectarian rivalry. There is no surer preparation for bitter strife, heart-burnings, and hatred, than these pseudo unionistic combinations. One union revival has torn religious communities into hateful divisions which have never been healed… And none have suffered so much by these arts, as our Lutheran people, who, free from guile themselves, did not suspect it in others. Well might we ask with the 'Apology:' 'Are they not ashamed to talk in such terms of love, and preach love, and cry love, and do everything but practice love!

In conclusion we wish to present the testimony of some of the most eminent divines of the Methodist Episcopal Church. Of all others they will certainly not be accused of being prejudiced against modern revivals. And of all modern revivals, those conducted by the Evangelists, Moody and Sankey, were probably the least objectionable. At the close of the celebrated "Hippodrome revival," in New York City, conducted by Messrs. Moody and Sankey, in the spring of 1876, the Methodist Episcopal ministers, at a stated meeting, reviewed the revival and its results. The *New York Herald* gave the following account of their meeting, which we copy from Rev. Trabert's tract:

The Methodist ministers had under consideration the question of the value of special evangelistic efforts in regular Church work, with particular reference to the number of Hippodrome converts who may have united with their churches. For two weeks a member of the Hippodrome committee had distributed cards to the preachers with the names of persons who declared themselves converts of Mr. Moody's meetings. Four thousand had been reported as the fruits of the ten weeks special effort. Ten thousand inquirers had been reported.

Dr. Robert Crook took the ground that special evangelistic agencies are not necessary, and that the work is more permanent and successful when performed through the regular church channels. Rev. J. Selleck, of Lexington avenue church, had sent about sixty of his members as singers and ushers, and had not only received not a single convert from that place into his church, but had been unable to gather in the members he gave them, who were still running here and there after sensations! Rev. J. F. Richmond had received a number of cards, and could report two or three converts who would unite with his church, but in connection with Hope Chapel he had not much success. He had gone to five places indicated on the cards as residences of converts, but could find none of them. This was his experience also with many others whom he had sought out. Rev. John Jones had received many cards, and had found out some direct frauds, and many others nearly so. He did discover eight persons converted at Mr. Moody's meetings, six of whom would unite with his church. Rev. C. G. Goss did not think any one effort or kind of effort was going to convert the world. We could not measure religious efforts by financial or numerical measurements. As to the general question, he had the history of ten city churches always known as revival churches. In 1869 they had reported one hundred probationers each. In 1870 they reported a net loss of five hundred, making, with the probationers reported, a loss of fifteen hundred in one year, in ten churches.

Bedford street church was an example of a revival church: St. Paul's the opposite. The former reported, in twenty years, twenty-five hundred probationers. But the increase of her membership to that period was only one hundred and twenty-eight. He could not account for this. On the other hand, St. Paul's reported four hundred and forty-eight probationers, for twenty-five years, and her increase in membership has been two hundred and eighty-six. This was to him an argument in favor of regular church work.

27

Revivals: The Billy Sunday Type

IN the preceding chapters we discussed the more old-fashioned revivals, as they were gotten up and carried on in the more emotional Churches, especially in the smaller towns and in the open country, as well as the great, well organized, professional revivals of which the Moody and Sankey movements were the most conspicuous. They had many imitators, such as the Chapman-Alexander, the Gypsy Smith and other campaigns. The objections written above deal with this older type of revivalism. The objections are just as valid against the newer type so widely in vogue as we send forth this new revision of The Way of Salvation.

The Billy Sunday revival, with its multitude of weak imitations, that set up their temporary tabernacles in city, town and village the land over, must also be discussed. In addition to the above objections there are even more serious ones against this latest type. It has all the weaknesses of the older kind mentioned above. Too often it lacks the downright earnestness, the consuming, unselfish, self-sacrificing zeal of the older movements. While we objected seriously to what Moody and his followers left out, to the superficial and emotional appeals and methods, we could not doubt the deep sincerity and the soul-consecration of Dwight L. Moody and those who were like him. Personally, both in his private and his public life he exemplified the life that is hid with God in Christ. We often wished that we might be as good and as godly as Moody was.

REVIVALS: THE BILLY SUNDAY TYPE

As to Billy Sunday. Insofar as he fearlessly proclaims the terrors of the Law against sin and against sinners, denouncing unsparingly the sins of the rich and great, as well as those of the common herd, we are glad for this voice in the wilderness. Insofar as he plainly preaches the need of heartfelt repentance that is evidenced by bringing forth its proper fruits, the absolute need of faith in the vicarious atonement of the God-Man Christ Jesus, the absolute need of renewal by the third Person in the Trinity, the Holy Ghost, the inspiration, inerrancy and divine authority of the Scriptures, we rejoice in his sledgehammer blows against the high-headed, pompous and empty rationalism and liberalism of the day. Inasfar as he scores, scouts and flays the saloon and all its disgusting spawn, impurity in high and in low places, hypocrisy in pulpit and in pew and shoddy pretentiousness wherever found, we say Amen. Inasfar as he mercilessly exposes and ex coriates the shallowness, the sham and the fraud of modern substitutes for Christianity and their empty-headed dupes, we glory in his demolishments. We appreciate truth wherever we find it. We do not condemn the good with the bad. Neither are we ready to deny that any good comes out of these Sunday campaigns.

But all this does not make us shut our eyes to the glaring faults of Sunday and his cheaper imitators. His ridiculing and condemning of the rank and file of preachers and Churches — especially of those who do not agree with him. His ignoring and belittling of the Sacraments and of Catechization, his shocking, irreverent manner of handling the Word of God, of the Bible characters, of the name of God and of Christ; his profane prayers and his whole undignified and clownish demeanor while preaching or praying, all this we deplore and abhor. By all this he wounds the blessed Christ in the house of His friends and brings the holy and the divine into contempt. By these rude and glaring faults, he encourages irreverence and sacrilege, cheapens and casts contempt on all that is holy and does untold damage to the receptive souls before him. The whole conduct of his meetings is low and vulgar. The cheap jokes from the platform, the boisterous laughing, clapping of hands, waving of hats and shouting, are all more befitting to the cheap show than to a religious service. The singing, which ought to be worship, is all too often a burlesque. The clownish leader's aim seems to be chiefly to call forth bursts of laughter and applause. The songs are often the worst poetry. The showing off of the choir against the audience, of the men against the women, and vice versa, the grotesque at tempts of the men—and sometimes of the women—to whistle the air, the ridiculous apings of the leader, all shot through with shouting hilariousness—all this is certainly not conducive to worship or to bringing souls to an intelligent, a thoughtful, a serious repenting for sin and a clear, believing acceptance of Christ. How intelligent Christians can accept and endorse such a burlesque of worship passes our understanding.

And finally we cannot help but mention the financial side of this modern revival business. Billy Sunday is reported to be getting immensely rich. The Literary Digest of April 3, 1915, published a photograph of a check for $51,136.85[7] made out to Billy Sunday for his services of a few weeks in Philadelphia. The same paper figures out that for twenty-one short engagements the thrifty evangelist received $346,665.91.[8] Does not this look like making gain out of godliness? We leave it to the reader. We are sorry to make these strictures on modern evangelism. We sincerely wish it were not necessary. Our heart's desire is that all evangelistic effort might be such as will bear the searchlight of the divine Word. Then would we gladly endorse it and cooperate with all our powers. But we must prove all and hold fast the good only.

---

[7] With inflation, this equals about $144,908.50 in 2013

[8] With inflation, this figure is roughly equivalent to $6,324,052.86 in 2013

28

True Revivals

IN the preceding pages we have seen that the Church ought constantly to aim at keeping up such a state of spiritual life as to render revivals unnecessary. We have also admitted that, owing to human infirmity, carelessness, and neglect of a proper and prayerful use of the means of grace, the spiritual life will often-times languish in individuals, in families, in congregations and communities; and that, at such times, a spiritual awakening or refreshing is necessary. We have further shown, that the modern revival system is unscriptural and positively injurious in its consequences, and therefore cannot be regarded or adopted as a part of God's Way of Salvation. What then is to be done when a revival is really needed. What sort of a revival shall be longed for, prayed for, and labored for?

In the first place, let there be a revival in each individual heart. Let there be an earnest and prayerful return to the neglected Word. Let there be a devout reading and meditation of the Law of God, an earnest, persevering searching of the heart and life in the light of that law, until there is a feeling of guilt and shame. Then let there be a prayerful reading and rereading of the Penitential Psalms, the seventh chapter of Romans, the fifty-third of Isaiah, the fifteenth of Luke, the fifth and eighth of Romans, and the epistles of John. Along with this private use of the divine Word, let there be a like prayerful public use. In case of perplexity and doubt, let there be an unburdening before the pastor, with a request for instruction and prayer. This process will bring about penitence for sin and faith in Christ. Let it continue to be a daily dying unto sin, a daily living unto righteousness, a daily putting off the old man, a daily putting on the new man — a daily repentance for sin, and a daily turning to and laying hold of Christ. Such a revival is Scriptural and efficacious. It will not only put an end to the languor and deadness of the past, but it will preclude the necessity of future periodic excitements.

Along with this individual reviving, let there be an earnest praying and striving for a reviving in the whole congregation of a life that may abide. Let every service in God's house be a revival service. Let each worshiper be a mourner over his sins, each pew an anxious seat. To this end let the preaching of the Word be plain and direct. Let it be full of "repentance toward God and faith in our Lord Jesus Christ"(Acts 20:21). Where hearts are not willfully closed against such preaching of "the truth as it is in Jesus," they will, through its power, become "broken and contrite hearts,"(Psalm 51:17) from which will arise earnest pleadings for forgive ness and acceptance. Faith will come and grow by hearing, and hearing by the Word of God. Where the Word is truly preached and rightly heard, there will be a constant and scriptural revival. Each service will be "a time of refreshing from the presence of the Lord." In addition to the regular weekly service, the Church also has her stated communion seasons.

These, if rightly improved by pastor and pe ple, can be made still richer seasons of grace. In our Lutheran Church, with her deep, significant and inspiring doctrine of this holy Sacrament, with her solemn and searching preparatory service, every such season ought to be a time of refreshing. What an auspicious opportunity is here offered for special sermons to precede the Holy Communion, for recalling the wanderer, awaking the drowsy, and establishing the doubting! What pastor, who has a Christ-like interest in the spiritual welfare of his people, and who has used his communion seasons to this end, has not often realized that they are indeed times of refreshing from the presence of the Lord?

These communion seasons become still more effective and valuable when they come, as they generally do in our Lutheran Church, in connection with our great Church Festivals. Our Church has wisely held on to these great historic feasts. They have from the earliest times been the Church's true revival seasons. Church historians inform us that during the age immediately succeeding the time of the Apostles, when the Church was still comparatively pure and fervently devout, these festival seasons were the real high-days, the crowning days of the year. On these occasions the Word was preached with more than ordinary power, and the Sacraments were dispensed with unusual solemnity. Then the churches were filled to overflowing. A solemn stillness reigned over city and country. Wordly cares and pleasures were laid aside, and the great saving facts of the Gospel then commemorated were the all-absorbing theme. At such times, even the worldly and careless felt an almost irresistible impulse to follow the happy Christian crowd to the house of God. Multitudes of sinners were converted and gathered into the Church of Jesus Christ, while saints were strengthened and built up in their holy faith.

Thus these festival communion seasons were true revival seasons. And why should it not be so now? What can be more inspiring and impressive than these great facts which our church festivals commemorate? If the solemn warnings of the Advent season, the glad tidings of the Christmas season, the touching and searching lessons of the Lenten season, the holy, inspiring joyousness of the Easter season, or the instructive admonitions of the Pentecostal season, will not attract and move and edify the hearts of men, what will? What has the radical part of the Church gained by setting aside these seasons, hallowed by the use of Christ, His apostles and martyrs, the Church Fathers and Reformers? Is the modern revival system or the Week of Prayer arrangement an improvement? Can any modern self-appointed committee get up a better and more effective program than our historic Holy Week services, crowned with its Easter communion ? Assuredly no! There can be no new "program," however broad or spicy, that can be adapted to bless the saint and sinner, like our old order, following the dear Savior, step by step, on his weary way to the cross and tomb, and thus preaching Christ crucified for, at least, one whole week in a year.

Though there may be progressive Greeks to day to whom this preaching of Christ Crucified is "foolishness," or materialistic Jews to whom it is "a stumbling block," we know it is still the power of God and the wisdom of God to all who believe. We know that there can be nothing so truly promotes genuine piety, so well adapted for the conversion of sinners and the sanctifying of believers as this preaching of the cross. We do not wonder, therefore, that, after a comparatively short experience in the new way, earnest voices are being raised, in quarters, whence a few years ago came nothing but ridicule of Lenten services, pleading for the old historic Holy Week, instead of the new Week of Prayer. Not that we object to a week of prayer. We only object to the substitution of this modern week, with its diversified program, for the old week with its bible passion lessons. Thus then we see that there is abundant pro vision and opportunity for special seasons of awakening and refreshing, by following the regular church year.

We would not, however, claim that, in the present state of affairs, on account of a lack of proper understanding and churchliness and because of the unconscious influence of popular notions, there is no need, occasion, and opportunity for still more marked and general awakenings. The word of God speaks of "times of visitation," "times of refreshing," an "accepted time," a "day of salvation," "thy day." There are times and seasons when the good Lord draws especially near to sinners to convert and save them; times when His Spirit manifests Himself more fully in the Church than at other times. In His own wise Providence He brings about and prepares the Church for such times. Thus, when, from causes noted above, the Church grows cold and languid, He sends afflictions of various kinds, when people are made to realize the uncertainty and unsatisfactory nature of the affairs of this life; when by losses, diseases, bereavements, or bitter disappointments, God seeks to wean them from their worldly idols. Then He brings them to reflection. They "come to themselves." They are ready to recall and hear the Father's voice. They are willing to hear the long neglected Word. They go to the house of God. They listen eagerly. The Word finds free course. There is no willful resistance. The Word drops as the rain and distils as the dew. It does not return void. If now the pastors and people know this "time of visitation," if they realize that it is a "time of refreshing from the Lord," not gotten up by human expedients, they will quickly respond to these gracious indications.

Whether such times come in connection with the communion and festival seasons or not, special provision ought to be made to gather the quickly ripening harvest. It is sometimes well to make provision for special services. There may be a series of special sermons. The preaching must be, above all things, instructive, a plain and direct setting forth of the Way of Salvation. The appeal must be first of all to the understanding and through it to the heart. The exhortations and invitations must be based on and grow out of these instructions. The great themes of sin and Grace, and the application and reception of Grace, should be set forth with all possible simplicity and earnestness. This preaching of the Gospel and instruction in the way of life should not be confined to the pulpit. The wise pastor will give opportunity for all inquirers to meet him privately, or will seek them out to tell them the way of God, as it relates to each individual case, still more plainly. This will be a true revival. Only let the churches discern and use the times, when "Jesus of Nazareth passeth by."

Every faithful, earnest pastor, if he cannot always have living, earnest and consecrated churches, can have such seasons of refreshing from the presence of the Lord. Every such pastor in looking back over a reasonable period of service can point to such precious seasons in his ministry. Such seasons result in a growth of true Church life. The means of Grace, after such revivals, are more diligently and more prayerfully used than before. The Word of God and prayer take their proper place in the home. The church in the house is quickened into life and activity. There is increased liberality in the congregation. The pocket-book is converted as well as the heart. There is a revival of strict honesty and truthfulness in all business affairs. All tricks of trade, deceptions, imposing on ignorance, short weights and measures, adulterations, making money by betting, taking or giving chances of any kind, everything in fact that is questionable, if not openly dishonest, is abolished. Wordly companionship, questionable amusements, pleasures that draw the heart away from God, are avoided. Religion is not only a Sunday garment, but a living force that shows itself in every department of life. The world takes knowledge of true converts that they have been with Jesus and learned of Him. Such are the results of a true revival. In such we believe.

This chapter, together with the others on Revivals, as they are found in former editions of The Way of Salvation, was written more than a quarter of a century ago. Every word as it was then written is still true. The old objections against false revivalism hold today. But, as noted above, revivalism has taken new forms and these call forth new cautions and new objections. Times also change. Worldliness is wilder than ever; greed for gold is keener than ever. Temptations are more multiform and more fierce than ever. These are the times that try men's souls. The love of many is waxing cold. Rationalism, liberalism, unbelief and misbelief are taking on new forms. False Christs, false prophets, wolves in sheep's clothing, seducing spirits in the guise of angels of light are abroad in every nook and corner of the land. Their bold assertions, insinuating slanders, scientific sophisms, seemingly scholarly arguments against revelation and against revealed truth, sugar-coated heresies, all backed up by organizations, associations and names that carry weight in circles of culture are indeed calculated to deceive the very elect. Satan is seemingly winning out.

The proportion of men earnestly loyal to the Church is said to be growing smaller from year to year. A spirit of panic has taken hold of many parts of the Church itself. In various quarters the old, unpalatable, humiliating truths of the divine Word are toned down more and more, until there is little left in the professedly Christian messages of the pulpit and the Church, press to which the easy going and impenitent worldling could object. The prophets are prophesying smooth things. They are to those that hear like a lovely voice and like one that can play well on an instrument. The teaching of God's Law, of His holy wrath against sin and unbelief, of judgment and righteous retribution in the world to come, is slurred over, silenced and denied as unworthy of consideration in this enlightened age. And so souls are rocked into a deeper sleep of self-security in sin. In more earnest circles in the church the incoming flood of worldliness and unbelief is deeply deplored and there is a nervous conviction that something must be done to stem the dangerous tide and save the ship of the Church from going down. These fearsome souls plan for, pray for and are willing for any kind of an evangelistic revival that promises relief. Shall we blame them?

What of us Lutherans? Our people are made of the same clay as others. They have the same human heart, deceitful above all things and desperately wicked. They are by no means immune to the danger of the spirit of the age. We have been in the habit of boasting of our progress. With hundreds of thousands of Lutherans coming into our land from the old world every year, why should not we grow even in spite of our many losses at home. But now the Lutheran immigration has practically ceased. What proportion of those who came over in our good years have we gathered into our local congregations? How many are the ungathered Lutherans all around us? And what about the thousands of other unchurched and unsaved souls living and dying under the very shadow of our churches? And what of the spiritual life in our congregations? How does it compare with the life in the congregations planted and pastored by the early fathers from Halle, who in the providence of God founded the Lutheran Church on our shores? Are not the blight and frost of our age upon us also? Do not our congregations need an awakening? Does not the whole Lutheran Church need to be revived? Has our great church no responsibility for the heathen in America? Have we no share in halting the heathenizing of our cities and our soil? If special efforts are needed to save the souls and so to save the cities and the common wealths are we to sit by idly and criticise what others are doing? "Is it nothing to you that these all pass by?" No, no. We too must do our part to save our churches and our communities; to save America.

We claim that we have a purer, a more consistently scriptural theology than others. And if this book is true our claim is right. Therefore we have a better message than others. To whomsoever much is given of him will much be required. Ours is the greater responsibility. We need to preach better. Our sermons must awaken the spiritually drowsy and dead. We must expect conversions. We need to be alive, aflame with love for Christ and for the souls He has redeemed. We must pray more. Thus can we have constant revival, constant quickening and refreshing in our churches. So will our congregations become praying churches. My House shall be called a house of prayer And then to reach as many as we can of the unsaved masses, let us not be afraid to take our good message to them where they are, preaching, as true soul seekers, from house to house, but also preaching in all public places, out of doors, wherever we can get a hearing. Let us not be afraid to take our singers, our grip-organs, our cornetists and our flute-players with us; sing what the people can sing and bring to the hearers a warm, gripping, instructive, inviting message from God. At auspicious seasons let us have a succession of services in our churches.

Let us not hesitate to use the press and the printed hand-bill and if need be to get the best preacher possible to assist, and so let us make the services popular and attractive with the very best music and then go after souls with the living and life-giving word. Let there be invitation and opportunity for private interviews with the pastor. Let there be pressing invitations, both private and public for all to join Adult Bible and Catechetical classes. Here is an evangelistic agency that our church ought to use everywhere and uses all too rarely. With our view of what the Bible is and what the Spirit does through it, we certainly ought to be the strongest advocates of Adult Bible classes. Are we?! We ought to have the largest classes. Do we? If not, why not? Here is a divine agency for wooing the sinner with the Word, and for teaching the way of God more clearly. In these classes the teacher ought not to preach. These ought to be frank and free conferences, where all can confer with each other, where everyone may unload his questions, his objections and his doubts; where everyone may ask for more information and for further light. With the right teacher such Bible classes can become powerful agencies for the winning and edifying of souls, as well as for training church workers.

For the unconfirmed adults, we ought to have catechetical classes much after the same model as the Bible classes. The adults ought not to be required to memorize the catechism like children. The great truths of the catechism ought to be made plain and ought to be freely discussed. This, too, should be a frank and free conferring together with encouragement for the unloading of doubts and of anything that may be on the mind of anyone. All the members of the church ought to be constantly instructed and urged to invite, call for and bring the unchurched, with whom they can get in contact during the week, to such Bible and catechetical classes. The earnest pastor will be most happy to follow up such invitations given by his members. We know of Lutheran Churches that gain most of their members from the outside through these agencies. It may be well to have a blank application card to be signed by those who may be persuaded to come. Again we ask; why is this blessed evangelistic agency so little used by our pastors! Let this be the new evangelism in our Lutheran Churches. Where rightly used God will assuredly bless it. Revive Thy work, O God among us. In the midst of the years revive Thy work.

29

Conclusion

WITH this chapter we conclude our studies of the Way of Salvation. They have been extended much beyond our original purpose. As we remarked in the beginning, we have written for plain people; for those who, surrounded by all forms and varieties of belief, unbelief, and misbelief, are often attacked, questioned and perplexed as to their faith, and their reasons for holding it. Our object has been to assist our unpretentious people always to be ready to give an answer to those who ask a reason for the hope that is in them. We also remarked in the beginning that there often come to our people arrogant and self- righteous persons, who say "the Lutheran Church has no religion," that it "does not bring its members into the light," and does not "believe in or insist on personal salvation."

Unfortunately there are only too many Lutherans who do not know how to answer such bold and baseless assertions. Sometimes they apologize for being Lutherans, and timidly hope that they still may find salvation even in their own Church! Many also have been persuaded to abandon the Church and faith of their fathers to find more light and religion elsewhere. After having been wrought upon and strangely affected by human and unscriptural methods, after they have experienced some new sensations, they proclaim to the world that now they have found the light which they could never find in the Lutheran Church! And thus not a few of our simple-minded and unreflecting people are led to depart from the faith and follow strange delusions. Our people need to be better informed about their own Church. When they come to understand what that Church is, and what she teaches, they will "no longer be children, tossed to and fro by the waves and carried about by every wind of doctrine, by human cunning, by craftiness in deceitful schemes" (Ephesians 4:14). It is to assist them to such an understanding and appreciation of the truth as it is in Jesus, and is confessed by our Church, that we have written these pages. If they have strengthened any who are weak in the faith, removed any doubts and perplexities, established any who wavered and made anyone love the Church and her great Head more, we are more than repaid.

Whatever may have been the effect of reading these chapters, the writing of them has made the Church of the Reformation, her faith and practices, more precious than ever to the writer. He has become more and more convinced that what Rome stigmatized as "Lutheranism" is nothing else than the pure and simple Gospel of our Lord and Savior Jesus Christ. Let us take a rapid backward glance. We see that the Lutheran Church grasps fully and accepts unreservedly the whole sad and unwelcome doctrine of sin. She believes all that is written as to the deep-going and far-reaching consequences of sin—that every soul comes into this world infected with this fearful malady, and, therefore, unfit for the kingdom of God, and under condemnation. She believes therefore that every human being, down to the youngest infant, must have its nature changed before it can be saved. The necessity of this change is absolute and without exception. In the very beginning, therefore, we see that no Church places the necessity of personal renewal and salvation on higher ground than does the Lutheran Church.

She believes that our blessed Savior has appointed a means, a channel, a vehicle, by and through which His Holy Spirit conveys renewing Grace to the heart of the tender infant, and makes it a lamb of His flock. She believes that where Christ's Sacrament of holy Baptism—which is the means referred to—does not reach a child, His Spirit can and will reach and renew it in some way not made known to us. She believes that the beginning of the new life in a child is a spiritual birth; that this young and feeble life needs nourishment and fostering care for its healthy development; that it is the duty of Christian parents to see to this; that the Sunday-school and catechetical class are helps offered to the parents by the Church.

She believes that by this nourishing of the divine life in the family and in the Church, "with the sincere milk of God's Word,"(1 Peter 2:2) the baptismal covenant can be kept unbroken, and the divine life developed and increased more and more. After careful instruction in the home and Church, if there is due evidence that there is grace in the heart, that penitence and faith, which are the elements of the new life, are really present, she admits her children to the communion of the body and blood of Christ, by the beautiful and significant rite of confirmation.

The scriptural doctrine of Christ's holy Sacrament of the Altar, which our Church holds and sets forth, and the solemn, searching preparatory service which she connects with it, make it truly calculated to strengthen the child of God, and unite him closer to Christ. Our Church insists that the whole life of the believer, in the fellowship of the Savior and of His people, is to be a "growth in Grace and in knowledge"(2 Peter 3:18). In this, also the believer is wonderfully assisted by our teachings concerning the efficacy of the Word of God as a means of Grace, a vehicle and instrument of the Holy Spirit. He is further comforted and quickened by that precious doctrine of justification by faith in Jesus Christ. He is encouraged to press forward to the mark, to purify himself more and more, to become more and more active, earnest and consecrated by what the Church teaches of sanctification.

Nor does the Church overlook or forget the sad fact that many—often through the fault of those who ought to be their spiritual guides in the home and Church—lapse from their baptismal covenant, or forget their confirmation vows, and thus fall back into an impenitent state. She insists on the absolute necessity of conversion or turning back, for all such. She does not, however, expend all her energies in proclaiming its necessity, but also sets forth and makes plain the nature of conversion, and the means and methods of bringing it about.

While the Church would, first of all, use every endeavor to preclude the necessity of conversion, by bringing the children to Jesus that He may receive and bless them through His own sacrament; and while she would use all diligence and watchfulness to keep them true to Christ in their baptismal covenant, yet, when they do fall away, she solemnly assures them that except they repent and be converted, they will eternally perish. And if this lamentable backsliding should take place more or less with a large portion of a congregation, our Church prays and labors for a revival. While she repudiates and abhors all that is unscriptural, and therefore dangerous, in the modern revival system, she yet appreciates and gives thanks for every "time of refreshing from the Lord."

Yes, the Lutheran Church does believe in salvation, in the absolute necessity of its personal application, and in eternal perdition to everyone who will not come to God in His own way of salvation—through Jesus Christ. And thus the Lutheran system is a complete system. It takes in everything revealed in the Word. It teaches to observe all things that Christ has commanded. It declares the whole counsel of God. The Lutheran Church believes in a Way of being saved. She has a positive system of faith. Her system of the doctrines and methods of Grace is a complete, a consistent, a simple, an attractive one. It avoids the contradictions and difficulties of other ways and systems. It is thoroughly loyal to God's Word. Where it differs from other systems and faiths, it is because it abides by and bows to what is written, while others depart from and change the record to suit their reasons. It gives all the glory of salvation to God. It throws all the responsibility of being saved on man. It is indeed the highway of the Lord, where the redeemed can walk in safety and in joy. It is the old path, the good Way wherein men can find rest unto their souls. It is the Way trodden by Patriarchs, Prophets, and ancient servants of God. It is the Way of the Apostles, and Martyrs, and Confessors of the early Church—the Way that became obscured and almost hidden during the dark ages. It is the Way for the bringing to light and re-opening of which God raised up Martin Luther.

Yes, the nominally Christian Church had largely lost that Way. God wanted to put her right again. For this purpose He raised up the great Reformer. Is it not reasonable to believe that He would lead him and guide him and enlighten him to know and point out this Way aright? If the Lutheran Reformation was a work of God, does it need constant improvements and repetitions? No!

We believe that God led Luther aright, that the Way of Salvation to which He recalled the Church through him is the Divine Way. Millions have walked in it since his day, and found it a good, safe, and happy Way. No one who has ever left it for another way has gained thereby. To abandon the Lutheran Church for another is to exchange a system that is based on sound and well-established principles of interpretation, logical, consistent, thoroughly scriptural, and therefore changeless in the midst of changes, for one without fixed principles of interpretation, only partially loyal to the inspired record, more or less inconsistent, uncertain, shifting and changing with the whims or notions of a fickle age. It is to exchange a faith that satisfies, brings peace, and manifests itself in a child-like, cheerful, joyous trust in an ever-living and ever-present Redeemer, for one that often times perplexes, raises doubts, and is more or less moody and gloomy. A faith that is built either on uncertain and ever-varying emotion or on an inexorable and loveless decree, cannot be as steadfast and joyous as one that rests implicitly in a Redeemer, who tasted death for every man. We conclude with the eloquent words of Dr. Seiss:

We do not say that none but Lutherans in name and profession can be saved. But we do assert that if salvation cannot be obtained in the Lutheran Church, or the high way of eternal life cannot be found in her, there is no such thing as salvation. There is no God but the God she confesses. There is no sacred Scripture which she does not receive and teach. There is no Christ but the Christ of her confession, hope and trust. There are no means of grace ordained of God, but those which she uses and insists on having used. There are no promises and conditions of divine acceptance, but those which she puts before men for their comfort. And there is no other true ministry, Church, or Faith, than that which she acknowledges and holds.

Made in the USA
Coppell, TX
17 March 2022